Modern Library Chronicles

STORM FROM
THE EAST

MILTON VIORST

STORM FROM THE EAST

*The Struggle Between the Arab World
and the Christian West*

A MODERN LIBRARY CHRONICLES BOOK

THE MODERN LIBRARY

NEW YORK

Published in the United States by Modern Library, an imprint of The Random House Publishing Group, a division of Random House, Inc., New York.

MODERN LIBRARY and the TORCHBEARER Design are registered trademarks of Random House, Inc.

Map entitled "The Arab World and Its Neighbors" is reprinted here by permission of the cartographer, Jeffrey L. Ward.

Library of Congress Cataloging-in-Publication Data
Viorst, Milton.
Storm from the East: the struggle between the Arab world
and the Christian West / Milton Viorst.
p.   cm.—(Modern Library chronicles)
Includes bibliographical references and index.
ISBN 0-679-64330-3
1. Middle East—Politics and government—20th century.
2. Arab nationalism.   I. Title.   II. Series.
DS62.8.V57 2006
320.540917'4927—dc22   2005056165

Printed in the United States of America on acid-free paper

www.modernlibrary.com

2 4 6 8 9 7 5 3 1

First Edition

To Judy
and
to our friends
Leonard and Joan

CONTENTS

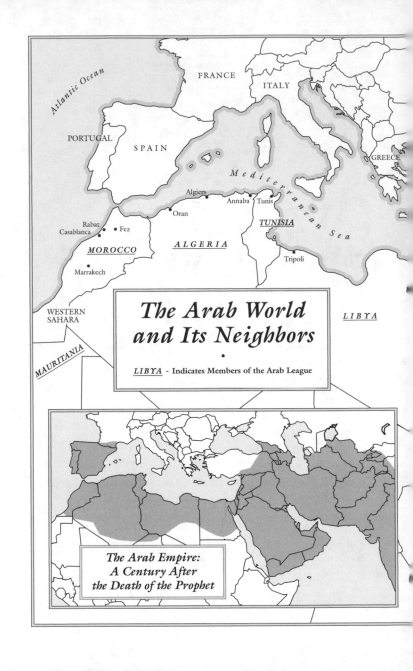

Atlantic Ocean

FRANCE

ITALY

PORTUGAL

SPAIN

GREECE

Mediterranean Sea

Algiers
Annaba Tunis
Oran

Rabat
Casablanca • Fez

TUNISIA

MOROCCO

ALGERIA

Tripoli

Marrakech

WESTERN
SAHARA

LIBYA

The Arab World and Its Neighbors

•

LIBYA - Indicates Members of the Arab League

MAURITANIA

The Arab Empire: A Century After the Death of the Prophet

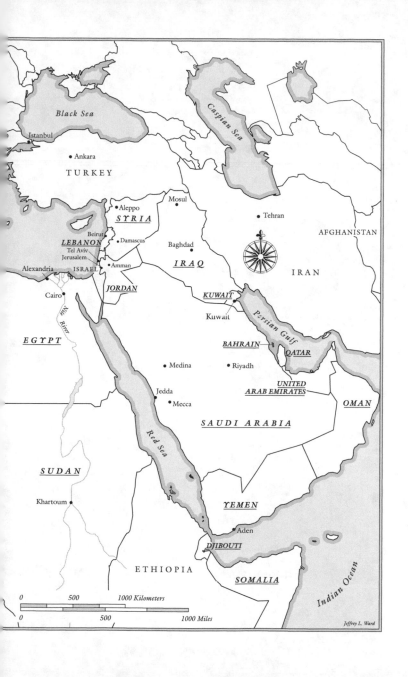

Black Sea

Caspian Sea

Istanbul

Ankara

TURKEY

Aleppo

Mosul

SYRIA

Tehran

AFGHANISTAN

Beirut

LEBANON

Damascus

Baghdad

Tel Aviv

Jerusalem

Amman

IRAQ

IRAN

Alexandria

ISRAEL

JORDAN

Cairo

KUWAIT

Nile River

Kuwait

Persian Gulf

EGYPT

BAHRAIN

QATAR

Medina

Riyadh

UNITED
ARAB EMIRATES

Jedda

Mecca

OMAN

SAUDI ARABIA

Red Sea

SUDAN

Khartoum

YEMEN

DJIBOUTI

Aden

ETHIOPIA

SOMALIA

Indian Ocean

0   500   1000 Kilometers

0   500   1000 Miles

Jeffrey L. Ward

PREFACE

This book, within the larger canvas of Arab history, focuses on the centuries-old contest for dominance between the Islamic East and the Christian West. The contest started in the seventh century, when Islamic armies organized by the Prophet Muhammad spilled out of Arabia into lands that were overwhelmingly Christian. In a series of stunning victories, they advanced as far as the Pyrenees in the west and the Bosporus in the east. In just a few decades, they established the perimeter of what we now call the Arab world.

Since then, momentous events have transpired, marked by ebbs and flows but by few interruptions, in the conflict between two civilizations. The Crusaders seized Jerusalem in 1099, and a century later the Muslims took it back, freeing the Middle East from Western forces for six hundred years. In the fifteenth century, Christian armies drove the last Muslims out of Spain, ending the threat to Europe on one of its flanks, only to face a greater threat from the Ottomans, who inherited the Arabs' sword, from the other flank. The Ottomans in that era captured Constantinople, the last great Christian stronghold in the East, and swept over much of eastern Europe. Not until they were halted at the gates of Vienna, first in 1529 and again in 1683, was the West relieved of the Islamic threat.

These pivotal events, though perceived from opposing perspectives, remain embedded in the collective memories of East and West.

The present stage of the confrontation opened in the nineteenth century, when the West, superior now in organization and technology, began nibbling at the edges of the Arab world. The practice, called imperialism, acquired momentum with the Ottomans' fall in World War I, which left the Arab heartland without a defender. Within a few years, the West's political domination of the Arab region was joined to its quest for oil, but its efforts fed a commensurate growth of fiery Arab nationalism. Whatever the military mismatch, the West has not had an easy time subduing the Arabs. America's war in Iraq, igniting an explosion of Arab nationalism, is the latest round in this long contest. To see it otherwise is to deny the evidence of history.

One clear lesson of the centuries of struggle is that both these civilizations possess enormous inner strengths. For the West to imagine it can impose its values on the East is a huge miscalculation. For the East to imagine the zealotry of its warriors can intimidate the West is naïve. Another lesson is that neither has the power to choose the other's course. Though the confrontation is likely to go on, both sides can profit, by lowering the stakes, from an extended lull. Notwithstanding its military superiority, unless the West accepts the East's right to determine its own future, the bloodshed that currently marks the contest will continue. Both civilizations will clearly be the poorer for it.

That is the message of this book.

I

MEMORY

622-1900

America's war in Iraq, from its start, did not go as President Bush's administration had predicted. Though the U.S. army captured Baghdad and Iraq's other major cities easily enough, and encountered little resistance in abolishing the detested regime of Saddam Hussein, Iraqis did not greet America's forces with the gratitude that they had been told to expect. Far from treating America's soldiers as liberators, which is how they looked upon themselves, Iraqis regarded them as conquerors. It was a characterization for which most Americans were shockingly unprepared.

Frustrated, the American invaders believed they were being misunderstood. The leadership in Washington had proclaimed repeatedly that its quarrel was not with the Iraqi people but with Saddam's regime. It had assured its soldiers of the nobility of their mission, not just to end a dangerous military threat but to wipe out tyranny and create the conditions for democracy. Wasn't that why the armies of their fathers and grandfathers had disembarked in 1944 in France, to a delirious welcome by the local population? In 1945, moreover, the defeated Germans and Japanese, taking for granted the victors' benevolence, willingly established free and democratic regimes. So why were the Iraqis so hostile?

Notwithstanding the political and cultural diversity among them, most Iraqis took the position that the American army was their enemy and placed serious obstacles in the way of its efforts to stabilize the country. This was the response of Sunnis and Shi'ites, Baghdadis and provincials, extremists and moderates, students, tribesmen, professionals, peasants,

Saddam's followers and his foes. By the third year of the war, many Shi'ites, perceiving an opportunity to shift political domination to themselves, had adopted with some wariness a strategy of cooperating with the occupiers. Iraq's Kurdish community, to whom the occupation presented an opening to long-sought independence, did the same. But the once-powerful Sunnis, with nothing to gain, waged a fierce insurgency against the occupiers. United in mistrust of the Americans, however, Sunnis, Shi'ites, and Kurds were all impatient for them to go home.

Why were Iraqis so much more hostile than America's defeated enemies had been after World War II? Why, unlike the Germans and the Japanese, did they impugn America's ideals and objectives? Why, after President Bush declared "mission accomplished," did Americans keep dying on the battlefield? Clearly, the leadership in Washington had initiated the war on the basis of a grievous miscalculation of Iraq and of the Arabs.

What the American leadership had failed to calculate, or simply dismissed, was Arab nationalism. Much as Iraqis were driven by sectarianism—Sunnis versus Shi'ites, Arabs versus Kurds—a long history of hostility to foreign occupation served as a bond among them. Yet American leaders, in deciding to invade Iraq, chose not to take this bond, and the deep emotions of Arab nationalism, into account.

Back in mid-2003, a few months after the invasion, when it looked to Washington as if its war had been won, President Bush was cautioned by French president Jacques Chirac about Arab nationalism, the power of which he had experienced as a young army officer in Algeria forty years before. Chirac told Bush that Arab nationalism was a rising danger to allied forces. "I cannot disagree with you more, Jacques," Bush replied. "Iraqis love us. We liberated them from a bloody dictator. The very few who fight against us are either remnants of the old regime, who are responsible for massive massacres and the use of torture chambers, or foreign terrorists, who hate life itself." The bloodshed of the years since then has confirmed how poorly informed the American president was.

To be sure, Germany and Japan, America's enemies in World War II, were driven by their own nationalism. But intrinsic to German and Japanese nationalism was a different conception of the United States, which imparted to both defeated peoples some confidence that the victor's presence, if not painless, might be benign. That was not true of Arab nationalism, which had embedded in it significant suspicion of, if not outright hostility to, the United States. America represented the Christian West, which had been the enemy of the Arabs for fourteen hundred years. The twentieth century had been particularly catastrophic for relations between them. Then, on September 11, 2001, in the embers of the World Trade Center, the gap drastically widened. History had not been kind to the feelings between Arab and American cultures.

It is fair to say that America, in initiating the war, had a duty to foresee—or, at least, to make a serious effort to foresee—what it would encounter among the Arabs. Arab nationalism was not a hidden phenomenon. Grasping its essence did not demand sophisticated minds, much less sophisticated secret services. The intelligence establishment's failures in *bringing on* the war have been amply documented. The blame for miscalculating what ensued *after* the American army rolled over Iraq must start with the president and be distributed among all those who advised him that Iraq's conquest would be, in the words of the CIA's director, a cakewalk.

America had available the wisdom not only of distinguished scholars but also of experienced diplomats and journalists. The literature was copious. Library shelves were crowded with basic information in books of history, religion, and sociology, even poetry and fiction. The books did not always agree—nationalism by its nature is elusive—but America's leaders cannot be forgiven for dismissing the admonition to know thine enemy. They were derelict in their duty to consult the experts, crack the books.

In an article in *The New York Times Magazine,* a revealing statement suggested that what was involved was more than neglect. It quoted a senior White House official who derided the "reality-based community," men and women who "believe that solutions emerge from your judicious study of discernible reality." In the Bush administration, the official told the writer, "we create our own reality . . . we're history's actors . . . and all of you will be left to just study what we do."[1] The assertion, corresponding with what is publicly known of the process that led to the war, has the ring of accuracy. Its disdain for data expressed a worldview that diverges from centuries of Western intellectual tradition. In precluding the need for information, it conveyed a reliance on what can at best be called ideology permeated by elements of the supernatural. It produced a war plan that left U.S. forces vulnerable to Arab fury, which they were not prepared to handle.

Let us admit that Arab culture is, in so many ways, distant from Western experience. American education pays scant attention to the ideas and events that produced the Arab mind. Even at their most diligent, Westerners have a problem getting beneath the surface of Arab society. But that does not absolve the leaders who chose to initiate an invasion of Iraq of the duty to take account of the culture and grasp what the impact of an invasion was likely to be. Arab nationalism, the "discernible reality" that America's soldiers encountered, proved a powerful force for which they were in no way prepared.

———

Nationalism, let us repeat, is not easy to define. Arab or other, it is not a doctrine. Nowhere is it rooted in critical thought,

intellectual calculation, rationalism. Rather, it is an awareness, a consciousness, a frame of mind. Nationalism can be
rash, even passionate, particularly in extreme forms. But at its
core nationalism is mystical. A nationalist need not be mystic,
since even among the most cerebral a space in the mind exists
for mystical bonds. Love is an expression of these bonds; so is
nationalism, a kind of love. But what other than nationalism
explains one's choking up over a symbol, a rectangle of often
tattered or faded cloth whose design identifies it as a national
flag?

All nationalism emerges out of a community's shared
memory. The memory is not necessarily accurate, and it is
rarely verifiable. It often embraces collective pride—or shame.
It may reach back beyond recorded history, but historical uncertainty does not weaken its hold. Nationalism is a mystical
attachment to historical roots that guides a common destiny.

For the Arabs, historical memory is the experience of a
community whose members, with rare exceptions, are Muslim and speak the Arabic language. Though they are currently divided into many sovereign states and many more
sects, they share an attachment to the Quran, the basic Muslim scripture. Almost all speak the language in which the
Quran is written. For reasons of history, the Arab world is geo-
graphically and politically divided. But their religion and language unite the Arabs. So do the lessons, correct or not, they
have learned from their history.

Ibn Khaldun, the Arabs' greatest secular thinker, understood the tie between history and mysticism as long ago as
the fourteenth century. He identified the Arab people with
asabiyya, a term rendered as "group feeling" in the standard
translation of his classic, *The Muqaddimah: An Introduction to
History.* Other scholars have translated *asabiyya* as "tribal bonding," "zealous partisanship," "the collective will to power,"
and "the sentiment of group solidarity that results from kin-

ship, blood ties and common descent." Each of these transla-
tions implies the presence of a mystical tie among Arabs. Ibn
Khaldun attributes this tie to Islam. Writing in an age of Arab
weakness, he laments that the Arabs, after Muhammad had
transformed them from hostile tribes to a religious community, were not able to make better use of their *asabiyya*.[2]

> Religion cemented their leadership with the religious laws and
> its ordinances, which explicitly and implicitly, are concerned
> with what is good for [Arab] civilization. . . . As a result, the royal
> authority and government of the Arabs became great and strong.
> Later on, . . . they neglected religion. They were ignorant of the
> connection of their *asabiyya*. . . . They became as savage as they
> had been before. . . . They returned to their desert origins.[3]

The experience of bonding that is at the core of Ibn Khaldun's theories took place in the *mashreq,* the Arabic word for the
area encompassing present-day Syria, Jordan, Iraq, Lebanon,
and Palestine. Geographers sometimes call it the "fertile cres-
cent." Though Islam was born in Arabia, the Arabs soon spread
their faith and their power to the *mashreq,* which became the
heartland of Arabic culture. Though the links remain strong,
the *mashreq* stands apart from Egypt and Arabia. It stands even
further apart from the *maghreb*—Morocco, Algeria, Tunisia,
Mauritania, Libya; the very name, which means "the west," af-
firms its distance. It was in the *mashreq* that the Arabs' collective memory and nationalism were formed. With deference to
the contributions of the *maghreb* states to Arab culture, it must
be acknowledged that the *mashreq* remains the Arab core. And
so it will be the essential focus of this book.

What, if anything, is special about Arab nationalism? Some
historians argue that nationalism itself began only with the
French Revolution, and that Arab nationalism resembles in
part the veneration of statehood associated with nineteenth-

century Europe. But in fact Arab nationalism barely resembles French nationalism. In different ways, Arab nationalism looks like the ancestral nationalism of the Chinese, the tribal nationalism of the Jews, the federal nationalism of the Swiss, and the multicultural nationalism of the Americans. The recognition that, by themselves, none of these models fit the Arabs, however, suggests a nationalism unique unto itself.

In fact, to understand Arab nationalism, it is best not to try squeezing it into the categories that apply to other nations. The expression itself creates some confusion. In the 1950s and 1960s, Egypt's Gamal Abdul Nasser promoted "Arab nationalism" as an ideology that aimed to unify all Arabs into a single state. Arabs call this nationalism *al-qawmiyya;* this book, to avoid confusion, will call it "Pan-Arabism." But Arab nationalism also refers to the loyalty, called in Arabic *al-wataniyya,* that Arabs feel toward their individual states.[4] Readers have also become familiar, more recently, with Islamic nationalism, an offshoot of Arab nationalism. Arab nationalism is further complicated by the fact that the Arabs, except fleetingly under the Prophet Muhammad in the seventh century, have never, in a political sense, constituted a nation at all.

But is politics crucial to the substance if, as we noted, nationalism is a mystical awareness, a consciousness, a frame of mind? What we do know is that, elusive though the definition may be, Arab nationalism exists. It expresses itself every day, often violently, in Iraq. And it is more. As the vehicle for the Arabs' sense of community, for *asabiyya,* it drives politics throughout the Arab world.

———

Arab nationalism, by any definition, was born in the arid desert of Arabia in the seventh century, when a simple trader named Muhammad brought the peninsula's warring tribes together under the umbrella of a new religion, called Islam. As its leader, Muhammad described his political mission as a response to twenty years of revelations conveyed to him by God through the intercession of the angel Gabriel. The revelations were received in Arabic and later canonized as the Quran.

Orphaned at a young age, Muhammad was raised by his maternal grandfather, then by an uncle, in the sun-scorched trading town of Mecca. "No waters flow . . . not a blade of grass on which to rest the eye," a contemporary observer wrote of it. "Only merchants dwell there."[5] Though a town dweller, Muhammad absorbed the austere culture of the nomadic tribes—hierarchical, conformist, resistant to change—of the surrounding desert. As a reformer, he imposed a new sense of order within the context of these values.

For more than a decade, Muhammad found few followers in Mecca. Then, in 622, faced with rising hostility among the merchants, he fled to the city now called Medina. Muslims regard the flight, called the *hijra,* as Islam's founding event. In Medina, Muhammad gathered his followers and led them in battle against the doubters. Victorious, he superimposed on the tribal culture a higher loyalty, uniting believers into a religious community, the *umma.*

Muhammad's genius lay in imbuing the *umma*'s secular needs with religious force. Much of his vision came from the Christian and Jewish tribes of Arabia, from whom he surely absorbed the concept of monotheism. The Quran speaks respectfully of them as "people of the book." But Muhammad was interested more in society than in theology. The vision with which he imbued Arabia's hostile tribes forged a nation. At its core was the *shari'a,* the body of law that fused secularism with religion, providing his followers with a pervasive guide to life. Though Arabs have since struggled with the idea of political nationhood, the *shari'a* remains at the heart of the Arab sense of community.

Muslims were expected to live by the *shari'a* within the bounds of the *umma*. Unlike Christians and Jews, who historically were free to observe their religion under any national flag, for Muslims the community was intrinsic to the faith. It is no coincidence that Muslims divide the world into the *dar-al-Islam*, the domain of peace, and the *dar-al-harb*, a perpetually hostile domain of war. Islam permitted the faithful, for tactical reasons, to observe truces with Christians and Jews. But its doctrine made clear that a truce was only a respite from the community's ongoing commitment to conquer disbelief.

Though Islam adopted the monotheism of Christians and Jews and respects their "book," the Bible, its attitude toward them has always been ambivalent. Islam holds both in awe. The Quran even instructs the Prophet, "If thou art in doubt concerning that which we reveal to thee, then question those [Christians and Jews] who read the Scriptures before thee." Over the centuries, Christians and Jews who dwelled among Arabs, speaking Arabic, have had social and financial burdens imposed on them, but, until modern times, they have lived in security and comfort.

Yet, at the same time, the Quran planted the seed of animosity. "Fight against those who have been given the Scripture and believeth not in Allah," it says, referring to the Christians and Jews of Arabia who rejected Muhammad's message. In another verse, the Quran declares, "Whoever seeketh a religion other than Islam it will not be accepted of him, and in the Hereafter he will be among the losers." Islam's claim was not so much that these faiths were in error as that its own superior truth superseded their doctrine.

The Quran, however, distinguishes Judaism from Christianity, to which it is more hostile. The explanation is that Christianity and Islam, being missionary faiths, with pretensions to universality, have always been rivals. In doctrine, with each treating the other as heresy, they are each other's mirror image. Judaism, as a tribal religion, was historically exempt from Islamic animosity. But from the start Christianity and Islam were competitors for global religious hegemony, making collision between them inevitable.

These differences no doubt fed the sentiments now identified as nationalism in both the Christian and Islamic worlds. Nationalism is not just communal love. It also thrives on its enmities. In both civilizations, the loyalties that emerged toward those within were complemented by the fears, envy, and even hatred directed at those outside. As bodies of faith, Islam and Christianity, notwithstanding their concerns with the divine, have proven extremely effective in nourishing each other's disposition to be terrestrial enemies.

That is apparent in the war being waged in the Middle East today. Though Saddam promoted a secularized nationalism, the fiercest opposition to the American presence has come from militants proclaiming their dedication to Islam. President Bush, in frequent public confessions of his own Christianity, has stoked the flames. A remarkably candid Pentagon analysis has recently argued that the "war on terror"—as the president named the conflict he has promoted since 9/11—was a cover: America, it says, is not responding to the threat of a rival power, as it did in the Cold War. It is "seeking to convert a broad movement within Islamic civilization to accept the value structure of Western Modernity."[6] This judgment, by the Pentagon's own analysts, puts its finger on what some scholars have designated a clash of Christian and Islamic civilizations.[7]

———

The Arabs mobilized by Muhammad after the *hijra* to Medina established their domination over all of Arabia, then launched an empire, heading west toward the Atlantic and east into Asia. In the decades after Muhammad's death in 632, they subdued Egypt, then swallowed up North Africa. They captured Syria and Iraq, and drove the Byzantines back into Asia

Minor. But for an inability to capture Constantinople and cross the Bosporus, they had all of Europe lying vulnerable before them. Adept sailors, they even advanced their conquests by sea, seizing most of the Mediterranean islands. Wherever they went, they spread their culture, absorbing the local population into the *umma,* the community of believers.

The Arabs' conquests brought many non-Arabs into the fold, but the dominance of Arabic, the language of the Quran and of daily prayer, preserved the Arabs' preeminence in this diverse realm. Muhammad, however, was the last leader of a unified state. On the one hand, political fragmentation inevitably accompanied the swelling of the empire, reducing the Arab *nation* to an ideal. On the other hand, the steady spread of the Arabs' language and religion enlarged the sense of Arabism and expanded Arab nationalism's base.

Muhammad's principal bequest to the Arabs was thus nationalism, combined in religion and empire, but he also transmitted a military tradition, more often than not directed against Christendom. The Quran's admonition "Begin not hostilities, for Allah loveth not aggressors" did not deter him. It was balanced by a commitment to *jihad,* a complex notion that includes the duty to spread God's truth to nonbelievers. Seven centuries ago, Ibn Khaldun wrote that "in the Muslim community, the holy war is a religious obligation, because of the universalism of the Muslim mission and the duty to convert everybody to Islam, either by persuasion or by force."[8] Many Muslims feel bound by this obligation today.

The barriers to Islam's growth into Europe were Rome in the west and Byzantium in the east, both deeply Christian. It was natural for Muslims to conclude that Christianity itself was the essence of the *dar-al-harb,* the domain of war. Curiously, the victorious Arab armies encountered little resistance to accepting Islam from the vanquished Christians in Asia Minor and across North Africa. Scholars agree that the conquerors rarely imposed conversion or punished those who declined to convert. Most willingly changed their faith, but substantial Christian and Jewish minorities, willing to concede Islam's preeminence, survived in an atmosphere of relative tolerance. In the centuries after the boundaries of the Arab world were fixed, Arab civilization retained communities of Christians, as well as of Jews, significant reminders of the culture that had preceded it.

Europe's Christians proved to be tougher adversaries than those in the south and the east of the Mediterranean basin. In 710 the Arabs crossed the Strait of Gibraltar into Spain, then followed the gaps in the Pyrenees into France. In a battle in 732 regarded as a milestone of history, they were stopped at Poitiers and began a long retreat. In Gibbon's famous phrase, had the battle gone otherwise, "the Koran would now be taught in the schools of Oxford."[9] Yet the Arabs remained in Spain for nearly eight centuries, and, with their armies also encamped at the gates of Constantinople, they continued to threaten European Christendom from both flanks.

The scholar Bernard Lewis describes Arabs and Europeans as "intimate enemies" in these centuries, though little about their relations was intimate.[10] In fact, it is generally agreed that they had little contact with each other. Arabs and Europeans sometimes traded, but social exchange was rare, and Lewis himself makes clear that the Arabs knew very little about Europe's philosophy and science, or even its music and art. Though the two were sometimes at peace—or, rather, in an Islamically acceptable truce—they also did a great deal of fighting. At the least, they remained sworn enemies. For nearly a millennium, Christendom felt besieged by a vigorous Islam. The confrontation left deep scars on the collective psyche—or, to use a contemporary metaphor, left traces in the DNA—of both peoples.

When its armies were brought to a standstill at the Pyrenees and the Bosporus, the Arabs' civilization was still at its apogee under the Abbasids, their grandest dynasty. Europe in the ninth century was in the Dark Ages of clerical domination and superstition; the transformation that the Renaissance would ignite was still far off. The Abbasid caliphs, the religious and temporal leaders of the Arabs, were much more powerful than any European king. Convinced that the halt to Islam's forward movement was more Europe's loss than their own, Arabs saw Europeans as barbarians, a judgment that at the time contained much truth.

Yet the judgment was also rich with hubris, derived from Islam's confidence that it had the answers to life's problems. Baghdad in that era took pride in its astronomers and mathematicians, architects and poets, and the natural scientists who advanced the frontiers of medicine. This was the Arabs' Golden Age, but it ended abruptly, leaving a nostalgia that is also embedded in the Arabs' DNA. The loss has imbued them with feelings of self-reproach and a nationalism notable less for its pride than for its anger.

The abruptness of the Arab decline is subject to diverse explanations. The simplest is that the endemic misrule and economic lethargy of the Abbasid era were quicksand on which a sound Arab society could not build. The Arabs' contempt for Europe provides another clue. Islam's refusal to open itself to a measure of reason, to acknowledge free will, to embrace the virtues of innovation and creativity, also exacted a price. Its closed doors produced a socially coherent but stagnant civilization. That its outlook has scarcely budged in a thousand years raises major questions about the Arabs' current prospects for resurrecting their Golden Age.

It is worth digressing to note that, under the Abbasids, a school of religious dissidents—called Mutazilites—challenged Islam's orthodox clergy to widen the intellectual boundaries of the faith. They were guided by the classical thinkers of ancient Greece, whose works reached them through Byzantium. In this contest, the clergy were victorious, reaffirming the immutability of Islamic doctrine, while the ideas championed by the dissidents, ironically, gravitated westward from Baghdad to seed the Renaissance. At a time when the Arabs were rededicating themselves to the austere desert code with which Islam began, the Renaissance was undermining Christian rigidities, imparting new dynamism to Western culture. It can be fairly stated that Islamic orthodoxy's triumph a millennium ago left the Arabs impaired to this day in their ability to compete in a changing world.

——

Some four centuries after Muhammad initiated Islam's great campaign of conquest, the Crusaders from Europe launched Christendom's first strategic counterattack. By then, Arab hegemony in the *mashreq* region had deteriorated. The Baghdad caliphs had ceded fund-raising to greedy minions and had replaced their Arab warriors with conscripted armies of Turkish slaves—Mamluks, a peculiar Islamic institution. Civil strife raged at the fringes of the Arab world. In 954 a Persian chieftain occupied Baghdad. By the time the Crusaders took Jerusalem in 1099, Christian forces had also regained much of Spain.

Powers even more menacing to the Arabs loomed east of Persia. The Seljuks, a tribe of central Asian Turks who had converted to Islam, captured Baghdad in the eleventh century, then took Syria and Palestine. In the twelfth, Saladin, a Muslim Kurd, founded a dynasty in Egypt and became an Islamic hero by driving the Crusaders from Jerusalem. His dynasty soon gave way to Mamluks, however, who finished the task of expelling the Crusaders. But in the next century, the Mongols arriving from eastern Asia devastated Iraq, killed the last Abbasid caliph, and razed Baghdad. Though Islam itself survived, and even thrived under the leadership of the non-Arabs, the Middle East was transformed, with the Arabs no longer at the center of great events.

In the fourteenth century, the Ottomans, a tribe that had followed the Turkish practice of converting to Islam, established their dominion in the east over their rivals, the Seljuks, whose rule was disintegrating, then advanced westward through the Balkans. In 1453 Ottoman armies finally captured Constantinople, putting an end to the eleven-hundred-year-old Byzantine Empire, and, within a few decades, they established hegemony over nearly the entire Arab world. Maintaining their pressure on eastern Europe, in 1683 they reached the gates of Vienna, the farthest advance in the campaign of conquest that Muhammad had launched a thousand years before. Their defeat at Vienna, barely three centuries ago, marked Islam's last serious threat to the Christian West.

The Arabs were subjects of the Ottoman Empire for four hundred years. Yet, in the Arabs' historical memory, it is hard to detect animosity toward the Ottoman conquest. They never thought of these centuries as occupation, and until the very end they showed no signs of rebellion. They expressed little resentment at submitting to other Muslims, whether Saladin's Kurds or the Seljuk and Ottoman Turks. To be sure, Arabs regretted surrendering their preeminence within Islam, particularly after the Ottomans took over the office of caliph. But they found solace in the *umma*, in membership in the Muslim community.

Even after the Crusades, it was the infidel Christians whom the Arabs continued to regard as irredeemable enemies. In the historical memory of Arabs today, the Crusades are a contemporary conflict. Their name for the Crusades is the Frankish Wars, and they still refer colloquially to a European as a *franj*, as if he were mailed and on horseback, wearing a cross on his chest. They think of the Crusaders' expulsion from the

Holy Land as their own victory, notwithstanding Saladin's Kurdish identity. Instinctively, they call Israel a Crusader state. Young Arabs on Baghdad's streets denounce the Western soldiers in Iraq as Crusaders, and when President Bush referred to his war on terror as a "crusade," many took it not as a slip of the tongue but as conclusive evidence of a new round in the age-old struggle.

For the four centuries of Ottoman rule, the Arabs had no collective identity as players in world events. The Ottomans had declared their sovereignty over the Arabs' holy cities of Mecca and Medina and, in laying claim to the caliphate, snatched away what the Arabs had considered their religious birthright. It is true that, as rulers, the Ottomans imposed no special burdens on the Arabs. They posed no obstacles to the survival of Arabic and Arab culture. They were fair in distributing civil and military offices, as well as places—few as they were—in Ottoman schools. If Arab society stagnated, moreover, Turkish society was not much better. But the price the Arabs paid for Ottoman rule was the loss of their sense of themselves, their national consciousness. Under the Ottomans, the Arabs as a people were simply absent from the world stage.

———

Christendom embarked on another grand assault on the Islamic patrimony, the first since the Crusades, at the turn of the nineteenth century. By then, the Ottomans were clearly suffering from the sclerotic symptoms that had brought down the Arabs hundreds of years before. Intellectual growth had slowed to a halt, the economy was lethargic, and the military had surrendered its edge. Technologically, Europe enjoyed a greater margin over the Muslims than it had even during the Crusades. The impending round in the global struggle—the Age of European Imperialism—would be a total mismatch.

Napoleon's armies were the first on the scene and, in 1798,

swept away Egypt's Mamluk defenders. Anticipating President Bush two centuries later, but no more credible to his audience, Napoleon proclaimed to the Egyptians, "You will be told that I have come to destroy your religion. Do not believe it! I have come to restore your rights."[11] The British, not the Ottomans or the Mamluks, drove out the French, as part of an intra-European conflict. But within a few decades, both Britain and France were back, gobbling up Ottoman holdings along the Mediterranean and beyond.

Starting at the periphery of the empire, the French took Algeria in 1830; the British occupied Aden in 1839. In the 1880s, France annexed Tunisia, while Britain reached deep into the Arab homeland to take the big prize, Egypt, followed by Sudan. By the end of the century, the British also commanded the waters of the Persian Gulf and controlled the sheikhdoms along its shores. On the eve of World War I, the French seized Morocco and the Italians Libya, completing European rule of the North African littoral.

By now, Europe, perceiving the importance of Arab oil to its burgeoning industrial economy, was hungry for a bigger score. The weakness of the Ottomans was no secret. Europe impatiently awaited the Ottomans' demise to take over what remained of their Arab possessions. By the time World War I was over, the Europeans had achieved this goal.

Yet on the scale of history, Europe's imperialism failed. Despite its superior power, the West's conquests provide a weak contrast to the seventh-century triumph of the Arabs, who created a new civilization modeled on their own tribal values. The Arabs did not so much rule over those they vanquished as absorb them. They spread a language and, more significant, a religion. European imperialism did neither. Whatever the strength of its armies, its administration, or its culture, it remained an outside force in the Arab world. It introduced the Arabs to new institutions and technology but left Arab life essentially unchanged. It can be argued that America's current designs in the Middle East—that is, the effort to replace Eastern practices with Western economic and political systems—represent another try.

Not all Arabs, in the era of Western imperialism, were persuaded of the benefits of the Islamic status quo. Appreciating the dynamism of modern values, an intellectual Arab elite sought them out by learning Europe's languages. Some attended its schools and universities. Many familiarized themselves with Europe's machines and flirted with Europe's political, economic, and social innovations. But, it should be noted, few challenged Islamic culture at its foundation. Few, in fact, do today. The Islamic world, it can be said, did not challenge the religious foundation of its civilization as the West, beginning with the Renaissance, challenged its own. Under Europe's imperialism, Arabs steadfastly refused to emulate those Christians who, in the seventh century, had traded in their own culture for Islam's.

Even in the heyday of the imperial age, only a handful of Arabs converted, notwithstanding the Christian missionaries who, under the patronage of European administrators, exercised a free hand throughout much of the Arab world. A few would-be reformers argued for a cultural compromise. Islamic Modernism was a movement that claimed that Islamic society could fuse the best of the West with the essence of traditional religion. But Modernism obtained little popular support. Arab culture as a whole resolutely shunned the basic values of Westernization. As it had under the Abbasids nearly a millennium before, Arab civilization stood its ground against the winds of intellectual and social change.

Still, by the twentieth century, Arabs no less than Westerners understood that the Ottoman Empire was dying and that change was inescapable. Though neither could predict where the situation was heading, among Arabs—at least among the

Europeanized elite—a recognition was appearing that strong measures would be needed to fill the void left by the end of the Ottoman order. Among Arabs who perceived the looming cataclysm, Islamic reform was not on the agenda. But a few broke a taboo to speak of Arabs' grabbing hold, after their long age of passivity, of their own destiny.

The shift in mood could not yet be described as a wave of resurgent Arab nationalism. As long as the Ottoman Empire was identified with the *umma,* few Arabs were willing to shift their loyalties. But, as the twentieth century opened, an Arab consciousness was indisputably reawakening. Many Arabs recognized that the impending war was, at least in part, over control of the fragments of the dying empire. A few surmised that the Ottomans' demise would offer the Arabs the opportunity to reclaim the role of player among the world's nations.

II

Revolt

1901–1918

As the new century was opening, Arab nationalism's rebirth was, paradoxically, seeded by Christian missionaries and European imperialists. The paradox lay in Arab nationalism's rootededness in Islam's age-old hostility toward Europe's Christianity. This hostility had been stirred anew by the indignity of Europe's growing military presence in the Arab patrimony. Yet Europe's imperial powers did not grasp the paradox. In failing to perceive a threat to themselves in Arab nationalism, they missed drawing an obvious lesson from their occupation of Arab lands.

Europe regarded the Arabs as the foe of the past, the Ottomans the target of the present. It saw the Arabs as a cipher in world politics, unlikely ever to be a factor again. With a mix of compassion and condescension, it considered acts of charity toward the Arabs a part of Christianity's divine mission and imperialism's noble duty. Any effort to revive the Arabs' collective self-awareness, the base point of Arab nationalism, seemed to be without risk, except to the Ottomans.

In the late nineteenth century, Christian missionaries, both Catholic and Protestant, established schools with the aim of promoting religious conversion. The missionaries showed a preference for Arab Christians, with whom they were more comfortable and whom they often converted from one denomination to another. But their work also spread among Muslims, principally boys. Over the decades, British and French colonial administrations built on the missionary base, organizing school systems of their own. The impact was greatest in Egypt, Lebanon, and Syria, the Ottoman provinces most accessible to Europe.

While promoting conversion, the missionaries also taught literacy, and when they introduced the printing press to the Middle East, it transformed the region's intellectual life, as it had Europe's four hundred years before. Through the printing press, they furnished Arabic textbooks to the schools. Ironically, though the missionaries almost uniformly failed in their primary goal of converting Muslims, they succeeded in spreading Arab literacy, fulfilling their secondary mission. This achievement exposed a growing Arab elite, disproportionately Christian, to European social and political values, nationalism not the least among them.

The nineteenth century was an era in which aggressive nationalism spread through Europe. The Ottomans had experienced its impact in uprisings in their Christian provinces, which led to the liberation of Greece and Serbia. In 1840, Catholic priests in Damascus, promoting the anti-Semitism that had crept into European nationalism, instigated an unprecedented massacre—though small by twentieth-century standards—of local Jews. Taking Islamic loyalty for granted, the Ottomans failed to notice how Europe's nationalism was finding its way into Arab schools. A few decades after the Ottoman Christians, the Ottomans' Arab subjects began to show signs that they were not immune to a nationalism of their own.

The Syrian Protestant College—today the American University of Beirut—was the most important missionary institution in the Arab world. Founded by Americans, it benefited from the perception that the United States, in contrast to Britain and France, had no designs on the Middle East. Throughout its history, it has been a caldron of intellectual activity among Arabs, and, not surprisingly, it was the site of the first identified act of Arab nationalism, when a few students organized a secret society aimed at promoting Arab independence. Though the masses were still indifferent, Arab nationalism's appeal was clearly rising within the Arabs' educated classes.

The Turks themselves, quite unintentionally, gave a dramatic boost to Arab nationalism. Enraged at the sultanate for presiding over the empire's relentless decline, a group of Ottoman officers calling themselves the Committee for Union and Progress (CUP)—generally known to Westerners as the Young Turks—embarked on a secret program to promote Western-style political reforms. Its constituency, however, was not the empire's diverse nationalities; the CUP was a movement of Turks for Turks. In 1908 the CUP conducted a coup, which preserved the sultanate but imposed on the sultan a constitution establishing an elected parliament. Ostensibly the constitution promised all the nationalities a share in the government, but that was not the Young Turks' plan.

The revolution's aims became apparent in the first parliamentary election, when Turks, though outnumbered by Arabs in the empire, wound up with a heavy majority. What followed for the Arabs under a CUP government was a despotism as severe as the sultan's. Generally more religious than the Turks, the Arabs were also upset by the regime's staunchly secular character. CUP rule revealed to Arabs the advantages of a nationalist movement of their own. All such a movement seemed to lack was a leader to bring the Arabs together.

The leader who appeared was Hussein Ibn Ali, who ruled the Hejaz, the Ottoman province that covered western Arabia, where Muhammad had once roamed. A small, erect man with a trim white beard and deep-set eyes, he was known for exquisite manners, and, in his traditional white robes and Meccan turban, he cut a dignified figure. Hussein's title, *sharif,* signified a descendant of the Prophet. His lineage passed from Muhammad through Fatima, the Prophet's daughter, and her husband, Ali, who was the Prophet's cousin. Sharif Hussein's family, the Hashemites, had ruled in Arabia for a millennium and reigns in Jordan today.

Hussein, as was the custom among the Ottoman aristocracy, had spent much of his early life at the court in Istanbul, where he was schooled in religion and government, as well as in the intrigue that pervaded the regime. An apt pupil, he conspired in Istanbul to weaken the sultan and, when at home in Mecca, to undermine his own kin who competed with him for power. In a report from one of the sultan's countless spies, he is described as "willful and recalcitrant . . . with a dangerous capacity for independent thought." When the office of *emir*, ruler of the Hejaz, became vacant in 1908, Hussein was fifty-five, and his dynastic credentials made him one of two candidates. The sultan and the CUP agreed that he was a schemer, but they considered him less objectionable than his rival, and so, apprehensively, they offered him the throne.[1]

The Ottomans' apprehension was compounded by the fact that the Hejaz was not an ordinary province. Because it was the location of the holy cities of Mecca and Medina, the Ottomans' sovereignty there legitimated their claim to the caliphate, the symbolic leadership of Islam. The Ottomans provided Hussein with a generous subsidy and kept him on a tight political leash. They also kept him under close surveillance from their large military base in Medina. The Ottomans, with German help, had recently completed a rail link to Mecca, presumably to facilitate the annual pilgrimage of believers; the line, however, also made Hussein more vulnerable by speeding up the dispatch of troops in case of trouble.

Even before his appointment to the throne in the Hejaz, Hussein seems to have made contact with Britain. The sultan, suspecting as much, had once warned him "to fish in healthier waters." With war in Europe looming, Britain feared that Germany, by gaining control of the Hejaz railroad, would imperil its access to India via the Red Sea. Hussein's ambition was not just to expand his authority in the Hejaz; he wanted to rule over all of Arabia, where he was already in a power struggle with an increasingly aggressive tribe, the Sauds. He figured that while he and the British had separate strategic reasons, they had common grounds for becoming allies.

In fact, Hussein had still a bigger dream: an Arab nation, free from the Turks, which he would rule. He also envisaged himself as the caliph of Islam, an office that had exercised little real authority since Islam's early days but remained a symbol—which the Turks had stolen—of Arab preeminence in the Islamic world. Hussein dreamed of regaining the caliphate and making it the linchpin of restored Arab grandeur. His vision of an alliance with a Christian imperial state, in violation of every lesson of Arab history, was an acknowledgment not just of Britain's power but of his own willingness to accept no barriers to achieving his goals.

Under the war clouds gathering in early 1914, Sharif Hussein sent his son Abdullah to Cairo to test Britain's interest in an Arab uprising. The British, perceiving Istanbul at that time as wavering between the Central Powers and neutrality, did not want to tip the balance against themselves. They foresaw an easy victory over the Ottomans in the event of war, but they also anticipated a contest with their ally France over the spoils of the empire. Unwilling to add Hussein's aspirations to the mix, they gave Abdullah no encouragement.

The circumstances changed after Turkey formally joined Germany in the war in the fall of 1914. The sultan immediately called for a *jihad* against the Western allies; Sharif Hussein helped to nullify its impact by challenging the sultan's Islamic credentials. In early 1915 the Turks, under a general

named Mustafa Kemal, who a few years later would transform Turkish history, won a major battle against the British at
Gallipoli and gathered their forces to threaten the Suez Canal.
Only then did Britain decide to take the sharif's proposal
seriously.

By mid-1915 the lines of communications between the
British at their Mideast headquarters in Cairo and the sharif
in the Hejaz were buzzing. In view of the Ottomans' substantial garrison at Medina, secrecy between them was vital.
Hussein, to widen support for his designs, sent emissaries
to known nationalists throughout the Arab world. To con-
solidate his Arabian base, he also dispatched agents to the
peninsula's major tribal chiefs. The message he confidently
delivered was that revolt against the Ottomans would produce an independent Arab state that would cover the *mashreq*.
The message was quite at odds, as the Arabs learned later,
with what the British had in mind.

In Istanbul, the CUP government, if not aware of Hussein's scheming, had no doubt that the empire's Arab nationalists were restless. Concerned about the loyalty of the heavy
contingent of Arabs within the Ottoman army, the CUP assigned the dynamic and ruthless Jemal Pasha, number two in
the Young Turk hierarchy, to Damascus with orders to set up
a regime that would deal mercilessly with dissidence. In August 1915, Jemal Pasha hanged eleven Syrians in Beirut. In
May 1916, he executed twenty-one more, mostly in Damascus. The victims were political leaders, journalists, and members of notable merchant families. Jemal Pasha provided Arab
nationalism with martyrs just as Sharif Hussein was about to
declare the Arabs in revolt.

The CUP's hard line placed Arab society at a crossroads. It
forced Arabs to choose between the Muslim identity at the
root of their centuries of service to the Ottomans and the in-

dependent Arab identity, uncomfortably linked to a Christian state, with which the sharif tantalized them. For the Arab elite, quitting the empire was far from easy. For the masses, it was still unthinkable.

In the summer of 1915, Hussein went into formal negotiations with Britain. The negotiations took the form of an exchange of letters between the sharif and Sir Henry McMahon, a professional civil servant who had recently been posted from India to serve as high commissioner in Cairo. The letters—four from each side—reflected not only competing objectives but major cultural differences. Most historians agree that they reveal the British as deceptive, the Arabs as naïve. After the war, each would repudiate the interpretation given them by the other. The disputes that ensued over the McMahon letters were central not only to the rise of Arab nationalism but also to the entire postwar history of the Middle East.

Sharif Hussein opened the correspondence with the questionable claim that he spoke in the name of "the Arab nation." He demanded that Britain agree to the establishment of an Arab state roughly within the boundaries of the Arab world and to "the proclamation of an Arab caliphate for Islam." To satisfy British colonial interests, he offered to concede Britain's preeminence among foreign powers within the anticipated Arab state.

McMahon, whose instructions were to maintain Britain's freedom of action, was so evasive in his reply that Hussein chided him for his "lukewarmth and hesitancy." No Arab revolt is possible without a clear accord on territory, he declared. While assuring McMahon he had no ambition beyond the lands populated by Arabs, Hussein stated that Arab frontiers are "the very substance and essence of our existence, be it from the material, the spiritual or the moral point of view." McMahon, after consulting with London, seemed to change his tune, answering with apparent concessions to Hussein's concerns.

George Antonius, an Arab scholar who produced the seminal study on the rise of Arab nationalism during World War I, described McMahon's second note as a breakthrough, "the most important international document in the history of the Arab national movement."[2] McMahon wrote that the letter "will convince you, beyond all doubt, of Great Britain's sympathy with the aspirations of her friends, the Arabs." Antonius interpreted the letter to mean that Britain recognized the independence of the Arabs within the frontiers envisaged by Sharif Hussein.

But whatever Britain gave in principle—if anything—it took back in McMahon's list of exceptions to the territorial concessions. One exception was the area "west of the districts of Damascus, Homs, Hama and Aleppo [which] cannot be said to be purely Arab." A second was the region in which Britain had treaty relations with "certain Arab chiefs." A third consisted of areas in which Britain was not "free to act without detriment to the interests of her ally France." Still another was the Mesopotamian provinces of Baghdad and Basra, where Britain had already "established position and interests."

Whatever Britain's intention, it is in retrospect clear that the first reservation opened the door to the Jewish mandate in Palestine, the second to the support of Hussein's rivals the Sauds in Arabia, the third to the satisfaction of French ambitions in Syria and Lebanon, and the fourth to the installation of a British colonial regime in Iraq. The exceptions left the Arabs with only a swath of the Syrian desert, and though this region later became Transjordan, it was a mockery of the grand state to which Sharif Hussein aspired.

The subsequent exchange, in addressing only minor points, left McMahon's second letter as the controlling text. At best, as an international contract it is extremely untidy, and the squabbling it produced over Britain's commitment has lasted to this day. At worst, it is a clear expression of British perfidy.

Almost all Arabs are convinced—it is embedded in their historical memory—that McMahon conveyed an irrevocable British pledge. The pledge was that Britain, in return for the Arabs' joining the war, would see to the establishment of a sovereign state ruled by Sharif Hussein, covering Arabia and at least most of the *mashreq*. The British say the letters contain no such thing. Antonius leaves curiously unexplained how the second letter was a "breakthrough." Scholars, rereading the letters, have found no answer to why Sharif Hussein swallowed the terms at all. Yet, bitter as was the taste they left, Arabs remember the McMahon letters as the beginning of a Western betrayal that would grow only worse.[3]

———

Armed with the McMahon letters, Sharif Hussein set out to persuade Arabs that defying the Ottomans was the right course. But, however he interpreted the letters, it was not easy. Most Arabs still saw the empire not as an oppressor but as the guarantor of Islamic order. Independence was taken as heresy, a secession from the *umma*, opening Hussein to the charge of *fitna*, provoking Islamic disunity. The nationalists in Damascus and other major cities, many of them secular, were too few to ignite a mass uprising. Arabia's Bedouins, on whom Hussein had to rely to fill the ranks of his army, had no quarrel at all with the Ottoman government. Whatever Britain's promise, it was clear that unless Hussein articulated a tie between rebellion and their faith, most Arabs would simply ignore him.

Ironically, millions of Muslims—inhabitants of France's African colonies and of British India—were already under arms serving Christian nations. They justified their affiliation on the grounds that they were fighting other Christians. But Hussein, in asking the Arabs to rise up against the Ottoman Empire, was calling for rebellion against the seat of the caliphs, against Islam itself. Few Arabs showed enthusiasm for such a project.

Hussein's ploy was to portray himself as more Islamic than the Ottomans. In a series of declarations in 1916, he insisted it was the CUP that was guilty of *fitna,* sowing disorder, in establishing a secular state. He accused the regime of disrespecting the Prophet and of transgressing the honor of Muslim women. He charged that Ottoman soldiers in the Hejaz had violated the fast of Ramadan and shelled holy shrines. The CUP, he said, had sinned even in having the Quran translated from Arabic into Turkish. Proclaiming that Arab nationalism was synonymous with Islam, he vowed that a caliph would head the new Arab state and apply the blessings of the *shari'a* to the entire *umma.*[4]

Though his pleas had won him only modest support, Hussein launched the uprising known to history as the Arab Revolt. His army consisted of a loose alliance of Bedouin tribes, most of them motivated not by the Arab cause but by the pay they received from the British. Numbering at most a few thousand men, they were lightly armed and poorly disciplined. Hussein placed them under the command of his second son, Faisal, who took the offensive, in July 1916, against a string of weak Turkish garrisons. Braced by Faisal's leadership and British guns, the Bedouins captured Mecca and Jedda. But the Turkish fort at Medina, with fourteen thousand well-armed troops, remained beyond their capacity.

As a war leader, Hussein never won the allegiance of Arabia's tribesmen. Since becoming *emir* in 1908, he had shown little aptitude for tribal politics. The Bedouins whose loyalty he had once bought with Turkish money he later bribed with British funds, food, and arms. But even as he proclaimed his vision of independence, his power in Arabia was being subverted by the tougher tribe of Sauds. The start of the Arab

Revolt was inauspicious. Hussein failed to awaken a dormant Arab nation.

He was no more successful outside Arabia. The Arabs of the *mashreq*, though outraged by Turkish atrocities, did not throw in their lot with him. The Arabs of Egypt, whatever their reservations about the Turks, hated their British rulers far more. By the end of 1916, Faisal's tribal army, had, with British help, bottled up several Ottoman divisions within their fortresses. But the Arab campaign was stalled, and the revolt itself showed signs of collapse.

Then, in early 1917, the British made a strategic decision to send not just arms but qualified officers to serve with Faisal's forces. Notwithstanding his lack of success, they had come to appreciate Faisal as a tactician and leader, and they concluded he could benefit from their professionalism. Assigned to serve at his side was the flamboyant Colonel T. E. Lawrence, later the celebrated Lawrence of Arabia. In his memoirs, Lawrence wrote of Faisal:

> I felt at first glance that this was the man I had come to Arabia to seek—the leader who would bring the Arab Revolt to full glory. Faisal looked very tall and pillar-like, very slender, in his long white silk robes and his brown head-cloth bound with a brilliant scarlet and gold cord. His eyelids were dropped; and his black beard and colourless face were like a mask against the strange, still watchfulness of his body. His hands were crossed in front of him on his dagger.[5]

Lawrence attributed to Faisal's Bedouins "secrecy and self-control, and the qualities of speed, endurance and independence of arteries of supply." Their forebears, in Muhammad's time, had been masters of desert warfare, ranging over the sands like ships on the sea, striking fiercely before withdrawing. Their mobility had defeated the more highly organized empires of Persia and Byzantium before reaching into Europe. In intervals between foreign enemies, the tribes honed their skills against one another. Lawrence was convinced that Faisal's forces retained the potential for victory.

In his effulgent prose, Lawrence makes clear that he loved and admired his new battlefield comrades.

> They were a tough-looking crowd, dark-coloured, some negroid. They were physically thin, but exquisitely made, moving with an oiled activity delightful to watch. It did not seem possible that men could be hardier or harder. They would ride immense distances day after day, run through sand and over rocks, bare-foot in the heat for hours without pain, and climb their hills like goats. Their clothing was mainly a loose shirt, with sometimes short cotton drawers, and a head-shawl usually of red cloth. . . . They were corrugated with bandoliers, and fired joy-shots when they could.[6]

Under Faisal's command and with the British at their side, these men confronted the less mobile Turks and turned the military situation in the Hejaz around.

Faisal's men hit Turkish patrols and cut Turkish supply lines, especially the Hejaz railway. These victories, though minor in themselves, set the stage for a surprise attack, in July 1917, on the Turkish garrison at Aqaba, a small port at the head of the Red Sea. In opening the port to British reinforcements for the army under General Edmund Allenby that was advancing from Suez, the victory at Aqaba changed the tenor of the war in the Middle East. Faisal joined forces with Allenby, who was moving northward to take Jerusalem, aiming to advance into the Arab heartland to capture Damascus.

His success gave Sharif Hussein the asset he needed to sell his cause. His reservoir for recruitment expanded beyond the tribesmen of Arabia to the thousands of Arab veterans of the Ottoman army, many of them sitting in British prisoner-of-war camps. The sharif flooded the camps with recruiters, while British aircraft rained leaflets on Arab units still deployed in the Turkish lines. With Ottoman forces in steady retreat, the offer of Arab independence took on new meaning. Hussein assembled an army of experienced fighters under Faisal's command, which proceeded to make a serious contribution to liberating the territory he hoped to transform into the Arab nation.

But by now the sharif recognized that Britain and France coveted the same territory he did. Recognizing that the territorial issue was likely to be settled only after the war, he also understood that the more numerous his followers, the greater the authority his voice would carry. The Turks helped him with harsh measures that alienated most of the Arabs of the *mashreq,* increasing nationalist ranks. But Hussein's most powerful weapon was Faisal's army, whose mission was not just to defeat the Turks but to seize and occupy Arab land.

Faisal's army was by now multipronged. Bedouins still marauded against Turks on the battlefields of Arabia and Palestine, sometimes raiding into Syria. But in the fall of 1917, some eight thousand of Faisal's veterans marched toward Jerusalem with Allenby's columns. Assigned to the right wing of the invasion force, the Arabs were positioned, after Jerusalem's capture, to penetrate deep into Syria. Allenby's orders to them were to take Damascus, but their unspoken objective was to keep Britain from seizing control of territory they considered their own.

—

Allenby's army, with its Arab auxiliaries, was at Jerusalem's gates when London first made clear that its territorial designs were seriously at odds with Sharif Hussein's. In November 1917, Lord Arthur Balfour, the foreign secretary, addressed a letter—since known as the Balfour Declaration—to Britain's Jewish community, promising the Jews a homeland in Palestine. Whatever his dismay, Hussein declared to Britain that he did not oppose a refuge for the Jews, provided it was within the boundaries of the Arab state. The British answered him reassuringly that the Balfour Declaration, whatever it seemed to say, was consistent with the sovereignty promised to the Arab people.

Hussein repeatedly stated his willingness to accept a Jewish homeland within the Arab nation. He sent the message to his followers, and even published an article in an Arabic-language newspaper urging Palestine's Arabs to welcome the Jews. If he had anxieties, he kept them to himself, knowing, with the war coming to a close, that a showdown was approaching. Tactically, he had two choices. One was to confront Britain directly, though confrontation held little prospect of success, especially with France, who owed the Arabs nothing, now beginning to assert its Middle East interests. The other was to rely on Britain's integrity, hoping that the Arab understanding of the McMahon letters would prevail as the framework of a postwar settlement.

Palestinians gave Allenby's army a rousing welcome when it entered Jerusalem in December 1917. Since Sharif Hussein raised no objection to the Balfour Declaration, Allenby, in his official proclamation, was equally silent. Young Arabs rushed to enlist in the ranks of the Arab army, and many Arabs in Turkish uniforms crossed to the British lines.

Meanwhile, over the horizon in Mesopotamia, the British did not fare nearly so well. Europe's influence had always been weaker in Mesopotamia than in the Arab lands to the west; likewise, until the final stages of the war, Arab nationalism had made very little impact. Mesopotamia's Arabs—or Iraqis, as they later came to be called—steadfastly supported the Turks. After the British army captured Basra in southern

Iraq in 1914, it did not advance much farther. While Palestinians were cheering the British, Mesopotamians were still fighting them in the trenches. The lesson seemed to be that, notwithstanding the promise of independence to Sharif Hussein, the Arabs mistrusted Britain. It was the mistrust, not the independence, that would prevail.

———

Then, after Jerusalem's fall, a shock of even greater magnitude than the Balfour Declaration reverberated throughout the Middle East. In November 1917, the Bolsheviks took over in Russia, and one of their first acts was to publish a sheaf of secret diplomatic documents from the archives of the czarist foreign ministry. Among them was the Anglo-French-Russian Agreement of April–May 1916. The new Bolshevik government renounced any interest in the agreement, but Britain and France affirmed its validity. The agreement has gone down in history by the names of its Western drafters, Mark Sykes of Britain and Georges Picot of France.

The Sykes-Picot Agreement was a clear repudiation of the pledges that Sharif Hussein believed Britain had made to him. Unlike the McMahon letters, whose language was ambiguous, the Sykes-Picot Agreement was straightforward in betraying the spirit of Britain's promises. Dismissing the vision of a sovereign Arab state, Sykes-Picot—the words, leaping out of the Arabs' historical memory, still fall contemptuously off their tongues—was designed as the vehicle for the segmentation of the *mashreq* into Western fiefs. It became the foundation of the postwar colonial system. Its terms, everything the Arabs feared, served as salient proof of the duplicity of the Christian West.

In fact, hardly had McMahon concluded his bargain with Hussein in 1916 than Britain turned its back on the letters, proposing to France that the two of them join Russia in making a private deal to dispose of the Ottoman remains. The timing suggests that at no time did Britain intend to fulfill its vows of independence to Hussein.

The Sykes-Picot Agreement was consistent with Britain's nineteenth-century strategic principle that proscribed the establishment of a strong Islamic state in the Middle East. Sykes-Picot not only cut the region into fragments, but also made sure that, whatever states emerged from the fragmentation, none would challenge European hegemony. It was a victor's blueprint for the spoils of the Ottoman Empire, designed to preserve Europe's power. To the Arabs, it was evidence the war was a new Crusade, in which Europe intended not their independence but their submission.

In the Sykes-Picot Agreement, Britain and France were generous with each other. France was conceded most of the Ottoman province of Syria, which included Lebanon, as well as a segment of Turkish Anatolia and the Mosul district of Iraq. The British received a contiguous swath of territory from the Mediterranean in Palestine to the shore of Mesopotamia on the Persian Gulf. Palestine itself was to have been internationalized, but this provision was superseded by the Balfour Declaration. Insofar as Sykes-Picot recognized the principle of Arab sovereignty at all, it was to be limited everywhere by concessions to Britain and France. Russia's booty was to have been the two banks of the Bosporus, Constantinople, and a segment of eastern Anatolia adjacent to France's. But the Bolshevik government, preoccupied with consolidating its revolution, took the high road by surrendering the claims.[7]

To the foundering Turks, the Sykes-Picot Agreement looked as if it might be a life preserver. Jemal Pasha, the tyrant ruling in Damascus, dispatched an envoy to Sharif Hussein with a letter arguing that Britain, with its mendacious promises, had misled the Arabs to rebel against Islam's rightful authority. Jemal's letter acknowledged some justice to

Arab resentment of Ottoman practices, and he vowed full autonomy to satisfy the Arabs' nationalist aspirations. But he insisted that the perfidy of Sykes-Picot reaffirmed Hussein's duty to return the Arabs to the *umma* and their historic membership within the Ottoman family.

With unaccustomed candor for an Ottoman chief, Jemal delivered a public address summing up his outrage:

> The unfortunate Sharif Hussein fell into the trap laid for him by the British, allowed himself to be ensnared by their cajoleries, and committed himself against the unity and majesty of Islam.... Were not the liberation promised to Sharif Hussein by the British a mirage and a delusion, had there been some prospect, however remote, of his dreams of independence being realized, I might have conceded some speck of reason to the revolt in the Hejaz. But the real intentions of the British are now known ... and Sharif Hussein will be made to suffer the humiliation, which he has brought upon himself, of having bartered the dignity conferred upon him by the Caliph of Islam for a state of enslavement to the British.[8]

Sharif Hussein, having refused to be diverted from his course by the Balfour Declaration, also dismissed Jemal's plea. Though Arabs might have recognized much truth in Jemal's eloquence, with the war almost over he was too late. Moreover, knowing the Turks, they had no more reason to trust them than the British. It might be argued that by the time Sykes-Picot became public, Sharif Hussein saw no alternative to following Britain to the end.

The British did not deny that they owed Hussein an explanation, but in providing it a few weeks after release of the documents, they were characteristically disingenuous. The Sykes-Picot provisions, they argued, "do not constitute an actually concluded agreement but consist of records of provisional exchanges and conversations." Denouncing the Turks for their intrigue, they commended Hussein fulsomely for seeing through the effort "to sow doubt and suspicion." Shamelessly, they declared that they would continue to support the Arabs "unflinchingly" in their liberation struggle.[9]

In June 1918, Britain, in reply to a statement of alarm by seven prominent Arab leaders, went even a step further in issuing a promise to the Arabs "to support them in their struggle for freedom." Called the Declaration to the Seven, it was written in a tone clearly influenced by the United States, which had by then become Britain's ally in the war. The American president, Woodrow Wilson, had earlier laid out his vision of peace in his celebrated Fourteen Points. In pledging that land liberated from Ottoman rule would be governed "on the principle of the consent of the governed," he offered hope to the Arabs, and Britain was not prepared to contradict him. But the Declaration to the Seven in no way repudiated the provisions of Sykes-Picot. In acknowledging that their priority was "the military operations in hand," the British aimed to avoid any distraction of the Arab forces then poised to march on Damascus.[10]

A few weeks later, when Faisal's army entered Beirut and hoisted an Arab flag, General Allenby, out of consideration for France's long-standing interests in Lebanon, ordered it lowered. Faisal, fearing a mutiny among his troops, protested angrily, forcing Britain and France to issue a hurried re-endorsement of Wilson's self-determination pledge. To restore calm in the ranks, the Arab flag went up again, but the underlying tensions between Britain and the Arabs were unrelieved.

—

After taking Beirut, Allenby was ordered by London to redeploy some of his forces to the battlefield in France, and so for the Damascus attack he moved Faisal's troops to the front rank. Spearheaded by the veterans of the Ottoman army, the Arabs never fought better. Allenby would have in any case prevailed over the Turks' weakened defense, but Faisal's contribution made the task easier. This contribution laid the groundwork for the Arabs' claim to have been a major factor in their own liberation. As a gesture of British-Arab solidarity, Allenby authorized the Arabs to enter the city first. Faisal himself galloped ceremoniously through the gates, surrounded by hundreds of horsemen.

"The Arab flag was on the town hall before sunset," wrote Lawrence, in an ebullient account of the victory, "as the last echelons of Germans and Turks defiled past. . . . Damascus was the climax of our two years' uncertainty. . . . Every man, woman and child in this city of a quarter-million souls seemed on the streets. . . . The men tossed up their tarbushes to cheer, the women tore off their veils."[11]

Embellishing on Lawrence's account, Antonius, who was not present, wrote, "Damascus was in a frenzy of joy and gave itself over wholly to its emotion. . . . Faisal appeared as the embodiment of freedom to a people to whom freedom meant, not merely an escape, but a long-dreamt fulfillment."[12]

But both Lawrence and Antonius, with deep ideological commitments to the Arab Revolt, had reason to exaggerate. Some seventy years later, during a visit of my own to Damascus, Bedreddin Shellah, who was then the eighty-four-year-old dean of the city's merchant elite, provided a more mixed version. Intellectually acute and articulate, he recalled the moment of liberation like this:

> When Faisal's caravans arrived, I was thirteen years old. Most of our people were bewildered. Only a few were nationalists. Many of our young men were still fighting in the Ottoman army.

The masses welcomed Faisal, but not out of patriotism. Most hoped the liberation would put an end to our wartime suffering.

We had contradictory feelings about the Ottomans. Because they were Muslims like us, we had not considered them a colonial power, and we counted on them to protect us against czarist Russia and European secularism. But they governed badly. Most of our people were poor, and only a handful were educated, nearly all in Islamic schools. It was a pity that, while Europe was having a golden age, life was so bleak in Syria. We saw the Ottomans as a barrier to progress and prosperity, but we parted with them only when they hanged our patriots in 1915. After that, there was no going back. Most Syrians thought it was time for a new start. That's why there was jubilation.

In late October 1918, two weeks before the armistice in Europe, the Ottomans surrendered, abruptly terminating four centuries of Arab acquiescence to their rule. As Shellah's words suggest, most Syrians were, to the very end, ambivalent about their Ottoman loyalties. His account is confirmed by other eyewitnesses who hold that Damascus was wary, even confused, as it dealt with the hopes for an Arab regime and the fears of a Western occupation. It is fair to surmise that, had the Ottoman Empire survived, Arab nationalism would not have surged into flames, and would likely have diminished at most to a simmer.

The Ottomans' departure, while terminating the rigors of war, marked the start of the bitter struggle for control of the Arab realm. Even as Faisal asserted his preeminence, French and British officials, backed by Europe's military power, were arriving to dispute it. Lawrence, now fully identified with the Arab cause, wrote forlornly that the capture of Damascus, high point of the Arab Revolt, "was the just end to an adventure which had dared so much, but after the victory there came a slow time of disillusion, and then a night in which the fighting men found that all their hopes had failed them."[13]

The Arabs were hardly prepared for the abrupt collapse of the old order. All of them recognized that they were no longer Ottomans, but what precisely were they? The struggle to create a new order was beginning. In it, Arabs would confront the West, but they would also confront one another. Sharif Hussein had pointed the way to the future by reinvolving the Arabs in the march of history. His son, Faisal, in establishing an Arab government in Damascus, sent the message that the Arab patrimony would never go back to being a satrapy of Istanbul. But the Arab Revolt, while giving birth to Arab renewal, had left Arab society with renewal unfulfilled.

The war in the Middle East had not produced the Arab nation to which Sharif Hussein had aspired. Nor had it given the Arabs reason, once the war was over, to scrub the memory of their ancient conflict with Western Christianity. Arabs, however, were all but unanimous in rejecting the hegemony of Western Christians as the replacement for the Ottomans. Having been exposed to the temptations of self-determination, they would not settle for a new form of subservience. But neither could they agree on the form their independence would take. The Arab Revolt had reignited an Arab self-awareness, but much more blood was to be spilled in the Middle East in the search for an Arab future.

III

DISILLUSION

1919-1939

President Woodrow Wilson landed at the French port of Brest in December 1918, just a month after the signing of the armistice that ended World War I. The liner that carried him was greeted by a huge flotilla of Allied ships. As he disembarked, giant crowds welcomed him, shouting *"Vive l'Amérique."* Paris, where he arrived by train, resonated with cheers as he rode with his wife in an open carriage up the Champs-Élysées. During travels in the ensuing weeks, he was hailed by adoring masses in London and Rome. War-weary Europe, it could be said, was prepared to defer to Wilson's leadership in negotiating the peace.

When the peace conference at Paris opened a few weeks later, the United States was at the apogee of its power. Though it had come late to the war, its army in Europe was more than a million strong. It was a creditor nation, to which its allies owed heavy debts. It was transporting food to a hungry continent. No less important, Wilson had earned the world's esteem in speaking out for democracy, stability, and international justice. Promising a nonpunitive peace, based on "self-determination," he conveyed an authority that was not just material but moral. To the Arabs, Wilson brought hope that the conference would scrap the sordid Sykes-Picot Agreement and grant them independence.

However, Europe, much less the Arabs, did not know Wilson. Born in Virginia in 1856, the son of a Presbyterian minister, he was deeply religious. He attended Princeton, in New Jersey, and returned there in 1890 as a professor before being selected as the university's president. He was elected New

Jersey's governor as a Democrat in 1910 and two years later ran on his record as a progressive reformer to win the U.S. presidency. While acknowledged to have a creative mind and liberal instincts, Wilson was also recognized among his peers as stubborn, partisan, and, most notably, self-righteous.

The economist John Maynard Keynes, perhaps the most acute observer at the Paris conference, said Wilson had adopted his father's religious worldview. "His thought and his temperament," Keynes wrote, "were essentially theological, not intellectual."[1] Wilson's own secretary of state, Robert Lansing, said that his vision "will raise hopes that can never be realized. It will, I fear, cost thousands of lives. In the end, it is bound to be discredited, to be called the dream of an idealist who failed to realize the danger until it was too late. . . ."[2]

Going to war had been agony for Wilson, but once he had made up his mind, he imbued America's participation with idealistic fervor. In contrast to the territorial gains that interested Britain and France, he was sincerely guided by a vision of a better world. His Fourteen Points, announced in January 1918, rejected as outdated the notion that the victor would dictate peace terms to the vanquished. Germany, vanquished, agreed to the armistice believing it would be a partner in the peace settlement. Being among the victors, the Arabs thought they had grounds to expect no less.

The Arabs were convinced that Faisal's march from the Hejaz to Syria had earned them the right to be seated at the peace table. Faisal was himself a head of state, ruling in Damascus. His strongest supporters, the Arab nationalists of the region, were demanding nationhood. Wilson, in declaring the principle of "open covenants, openly arrived at," seemed to reject the secret accord written by Sykes and Picot.

The president, in fact, had explicitly included the Ottoman Empire's Arab provinces in his vision. "Nationalities now under Turkish rule should be assured an undoubted security of life and an absolutely unmolested opportunity of autonomous development," he declared in 1918. When it was pointed out that these words fell short of self-determination, he later added that "every territorial settlement involved in this war must be made in the interest and for the benefit of the population concerned" and "every question, whether of territory or sovereignty, . . . [must be settled] on the basis of the free acceptance . . . by the people immediately concerned, and not upon the basis of the material advantage of any other nation or people." The Arabs were happy to take him at his word.

It seemed unimportant at the time that the United States had never declared war on the Ottomans, and that no Americans had fought in the Middle East. Nor did it seem an obstacle that the Arab provinces remained occupied, like Turkey itself, by British and French armies, whose commanders followed instructions from their own capitals. On the contrary, when the Paris conference opened, even Britain and France seemed to agree that Wilson was in control.

But in the end, the Arabs, no less than the Germans, concluded they had been betrayed. Wilson proved a weak reed, totally outmaneuvered by David Lloyd George and Georges Clemenceau, the prime ministers of Britain and France, who wrote the final treaties to suit their own narrow vision. In the absence of a strong American voice, the Fourteen Points were discarded into the rubbish heap of lost ideals. Only later did the Arabs, and the Germans, understand that Wilson, even at the summit of his power, had not succeeded in committing his allies to his principles. More significant, he soon lost whatever support he had in Congress, which meant he had failed even to commit the United States.

Much of the fault belonged to Wilson himself. He had

never devised a plan to translate his lofty principles into practice. It was as if he relied for execution on a divine power. The British and French priorities were to contain Germany's potential resurgence, then to enhance their respective empires; Wilson's priority was to promote eternal peace by establishing the League of Nations. Britain and France, though skeptical of its usefulness, were willing to indulge him on the League in the interest of promoting their own goals. Neither wanted to alienate America as a postwar contributor to European stability. It was not long, however, before they faced the fact that, because of Wilson's weakness, America had alienated itself.

In the end Wilson, in the charter of the League, provided Britain and France with cover to legitimize their imperial designs. As the champion of self-determination, he rejected the concept of annexation. He thought that, in endorsing "mandates," he was assuring the triumph of high-mindedness—the strong protecting the weak—over squalid imperial objectives. Wilson believed that a mandate would make its holder responsible to the League for nursing the society under its wing to nationhood. He saw the mandate as a step to political and economic self-sufficiency. But the theory was flawed, even naïve. Predictably, the mandatory system worked out tragically.

The Arabs were not interested in becoming European mandates. Faisal's Syria, coveted by France, was a prime candidate, but the Syrians insisted they had no need of France's care. With Britain's collusion, France succeeded in denying Faisal credentials as Syria's representative to the peace conference. He attended, instead, as the delegate from the Hejaz, his father's kingdom. Largely ignored while the victorious powers bargained among themselves, Faisal, in a Bedouin's white robe trimmed in gold, stalked the halls in Paris, often at the side of his mentor Lawrence, vainly addressing whoever would listen in behalf of Arab independence.

Britain and France pleaded with Faisal to accept the Sykes-Picot territorial divisions as the framework of the mandatory system. But, supported by his father in the Hejaz and his increasingly nationalistic constituency in Damascus, he saw it as a trap and refused to bow. The French also solicited his endorsement to separate Syria from Lebanon, where they wanted the Maronite Christians, France's long-standing protégés, to rule under their patronage. The British, further, sought his consent to the Balfour Declaration and arranged a meeting between him and Chaim Weizmann, the Zionist leader. Despite the pressure, Faisal answered that the Arabs would not retreat from insistence on full sovereignty.

America, in Faisal's mind, was in a separate category from Britain and France. Wilson was not seen as the head of an imperial power. Faisal hinted repeatedly that the Arabs, convinced of America's impartiality and goodwill, would, if necessary, accept an American mandate. But Wilson, recognizing the likelihood of rejection by an opposition Congress, declined even to have such a proposal considered in the Paris deliberations.

The closest the conference came to it was a recommendation from the King-Crane Commission. Wilson, in his early debates over self-determination, insisted to the British and French that the Arabs themselves had to be consulted about their fate, and he proposed the establishment of a committee of inquiry to question the populace directly. Reluctantly, Britain and France agreed to the commission, but they declined to participate in it. Wilson alone appointed its codirectors, both Americans: Henry C. King, a college president, and Charles R. Crane, a rich industrialist. When the commission was established, it was reported that Faisal celebrated by drinking champagne for the first time. In the summer of 1919, Messrs. King and Crane, backed by a professional staff, visited the territory that would become Syria, Lebanon, and Palestine, where they conscientiously collected testimony and documentation from the inhabitants.

Not surprisingly, the King-Crane Commission concluded that Arabs everywhere opposed the involvement of Britain and France in their affairs. It recommended separate constitutional monarchies for Iraq and an undivided Syria—a Syria, that is, which included Lebanon and Palestine. It also called for limits on Zionism, predicting the goals of the Jews could not be realized "except by force of arms." As a fallback, it said, the Arabs preferred an American to a European mandate, limited to twenty years.[3]

Though the report probably assessed Arab opinion fairly, by the time the conference received it, Wilson was no longer among the participants. He had returned home in 1919 for a speaking tour in behalf of the League of Nations, during which he suffered a paralyzing stroke. Without his presence, America's influence in the peace deliberations all but vanished.

Faisal, meanwhile, had gone back to Damascus to find his own role seriously undermined. Fiery nationalists, after decades cowering beneath the Turks, had emerged as the dominant force in the country. Damascus, moreover, had become a new, secular Mecca, to which radicals were flocking from all over the Arab world. They argued that, unless the conference granted full independence, the Arabs must once again rise up in revolt.

To these nationalists, Faisal, whatever his services to the Arab Revolt, was an outsider, a desert prince ruling in a relatively modern, secularized milieu. Faisal, seeking to mollify them, announced national elections; they produced an assembly in which the radicals dominated. The assembly proceeded to pass fervid resolutions declaring Syrian and Iraqi independence, rejecting all mandates, repudiating both Sykes-Picot and Balfour. Its ardor, coming just as the great powers were finishing the German agenda and turning to the Ottoman territories, dramatized the chasm between the Middle East and Paris. If any prospect of compromise between Europe and the Arabs ever existed, the assembly in Damascus shut it off.[4]

At this point Britain, weakened by economic crisis, called home its army in Syria. No longer able to bear the costs of the force, the withdrawal left Faisal alone to face the French. Retreating from intransigence, Faisal hinted that he might accept a loose mandate that would allow him to remain king. But militants in both Paris and Damascus, at opposing poles, rejected reconciliation. In early 1920, France, without British protest, landed troops in Lebanon, conveying its intention of pressing its rule over Syria deep into the interior.

Meanwhile, British and French negotiators formally met to settle the Middle East's fate. First in London, then in San Remo, Italy, they deliberated over both Turkey itself and the Arab provinces. No reference was made to the King-Crane report, and its later release made barely a ripple on Western consciousness; filed with Sykes-Picot and Balfour, King-Crane only added to the evidence in the Arabs' historical memory of the West's bad faith. In August 1920, the great powers signed a treaty on the Middle East in Sèvres, a Paris suburb. The Ottoman sultan, coerced by the British force that still occupied Constantinople, endorsed it in the name of the vanquished Turks. But by then, events had superseded the diplomatic process, and it was soon apparent that the Treaty of Sèvres was doomed.

The treaty was as punitive in its treatment of Turkey as was the Versailles Treaty in dealing with Germany. It shredded the Ottoman homeland, placing Constantinople and the Dardanelles under British control. It awarded western Anatolia to the Greeks. In eastern Anatolia, it created an independent Armenia and an autonomous Kurdistan, and it granted separate spheres of influence to the French and the Italians. The treaty left only central Anatolia to the sovereignty of the Turks.

The treaty also detached the empire's Arab provinces, drawing borders that established the mosaic of countries—Syria, Lebanon, Iraq, Jordan, Palestine—that we know today. The borders dissected the *mashreq,* the heartland that Sharif Hussein thought had been promised to the Arabs as a unified state. With a few modest changes, the Arab provinces of the Ottoman Empire were separated into mandates that followed the lines laid out in the Sykes-Picot Agreement.

The British took Mesopotamia, dusting off an obscure historical name to call it Iraq. They also gave themselves Palestine, defining it to extend their geographic reach eastward across Transjordan to the Persian Gulf. At the western end, they reaffirmed the pledge of a Jewish homeland contained in the Balfour Declaration. France, under the treaty, received Syria, in which Lebanon was included. The only Arab province of the fallen empire to obtain its freedom was Arabia; no one, in the era before oil, wanted responsibility for it. Sharif Hussein ruled precariously there as king of the Hejaz, while diverse rivals, notably the Sauds, governed the remainder.

The Treaty of Sèvres dealt with the Arabs as a defeated people, leaving them only the League of Nations as an instrument of redress. The League's covenant explicitly pledged—as a "sacred trust of civilization"—their ultimate independence. But Britain and France had never been enthusiasts of the League, and America left a void when its Senate rejected Wilson's dream. With paternal condescension, Britain and France established parliamentary structures in the new states, but in practice they exploited the institutions as simply another arm of colonial hegemony. There is no evidence that the mandatory powers, even in the long term, contemplated transferring sovereignty to the Arab people.

The aftermath of the Treaty of Sèvres was a series of events that startled the West. The Turks rose up against the occupiers before the ink was dry. The Arabs, beginning with Egypt, ignited insurrections against the Europeans that spread throughout the region, bloodying and embittering further relations between the occupiers and the occupied. America, having abandoned its commitment to self-determination, steadily declined in Arab esteem. Britain and France, as the crisis grew, remained confident that they could contain the anger their presence had let loose. But since the Treaty of Sèvres, Arab nationalism has remained the Middle East's most dynamic force.

———

Egyptians waited patiently for the end of the war to test British power. Among Arabs, Egypt's sense of nationhood was special. From the Upper Nile to the Mediterranean, Egypt has been united in government and religion, and even artistic style, since Pharaonic times. Though Islamized by the Arabs in the seventh century, Egyptians never gave up their national identity. Under the Ottomans they were consistently restless. Napoleon's conquest in 1798 triggered a fascination with the West. "My country," Khedive Ismail declared in mid-century, "is no longer in Africa. It is in Europe." But few Egyptians were interested in becoming British.

In 1882 an army officer of peasant origins named Ahmad Urabi had led a quasi coup against Egypt's monarchy, protesting not only misgovernment but the Europeanization of Egypt's affairs. An early expression of nationalism, it was the Arabs' first anti-Western uprising. Britain, alarmed that its access to the Suez Canal might be impaired, landed troops that defeated Urabi in battle and took away his power. It pledged that its occupation would be brief, but the British did not go home and, as the decades went on, exercised increasing control over Egyptian political life. Egyptians led the Arabs in Western-style reforms, spreading education and granting extensive rights to women, for example. But Egypt never accepted Britain's colonial rule.

When World War I began, Britain worried about Egypt's rising nationalism. Egypt was strategically important: Cairo was the capital of the British East; Egypt was the assembly point for the war effort; the vital Suez Canal lay nearby. In their hearts, most Egyptians still favored the Turks over the Christian imperialists. Britain imposed martial law on Egypt but at the same time tried to lull the country with a promise of freedom. While the war raged, Egypt remained quiet. When it was over, Egyptians—familiar with Wilson's Fourteen Points and the U.S. pledge of self-determination—were outraged at Britain's refusal to redeem its earlier promise. Egypt's nationalists insisted it was now time for action.

But, as the Nobel laureate Naguib Mahfouz acknowledges, not all Egyptians were nationalists. In his Cairo Trilogy, modeled on his own family, he draws a complex picture of a society divided between nationalism and religion. His heroine, Amina, pleads with Fahmy, her son, to stay away from violent anti-British protests. "How can you expose yourself to danger when you're such an intelligent person?" she asks. Mahfouz writes,

> Fahmy was closer to the heavens than he was to convincing her that he had a duty to expose himself to danger for the sake of the nation. In her eyes, the nation was not worth the clippings from his fingernail. . . . "Why do you despise them [the British], son? Aren't they people like us with sons and mothers?"
>
> Fahmy would reply sharply, "But they are occupying our country." She would sense the bitter anger in his voice and fall

silent. . . . Once, when he was exasperated by her reasoning, he had told her, "A people ruled by foreigners has no life." She had replied in astonishment, "But we're still alive, even though they've been ruling us for a long time. I bore all of you under their rule. Son, they don't kill us and they don't interfere with the mosques. The community of Muhammad is still thriving."

The young man had said in despair, "If our master Muhammad were alive, he would not consent to our being ruled by the English."[5]

On the eve of the Paris conference, Sa'ad Zaghlul, Egypt's preeminent parliamentary leader, appealed to Britain's high commissioner in Cairo for permission to take a delegation— Wafd, the party that later became the core of the independence struggle, whose name means "delegation"—to Paris to negotiate in Egypt's behalf. With Faisal already there representing Syria's case, it seemed a modest request. But the commissioner turned Zaghlul down, confirming Britain's intentions to repudiate its wartime vow.

Zaghlul responded by calling for mass support in the streets. The British banned him from public speaking and, in March 1919, deported him to Malta, touching off a wave of disorder. Students, civil servants, peasants, workers, even women joined in protest; rail workers cut tracks, segmenting the country. "Egypt for Egyptians," cried the demonstrators in the major cities. The disorders persuaded the British to free Zaghlul—in the Mahfouz novel, Fahmy is killed in a celebration of his release—but the demonstrations went on. Egypt calls these events the "1919 Revolution." It was not a revolution at all but it was an unprecedented explosion of popular defiance, and the first skirmish in the Arab wars of liberation.

After his release, Zaghlul outwitted the British and left for Paris. Unlike Faisal, he had his country solidly behind him. Britain had won Wilson over by persuading him that it was prepared to enact reforms in Egypt. But even if it was true, Zaghlul's objective was not reforms; it was an end to British rule, and Wilson gave him no encouragement. When Zaghlul returned in failure, the country fell into chaos; bloody strikes and street battles became daily fare. Dozens of British and a thousand Egyptians died. Britain exiled Zaghlul again, then shifted tactics. In early 1922, Britain offered solemnly to declare Egypt independent.

But, in fact, the British concept of independence proved a façade. Claiming to offer Egypt full democracy, Britain set up machinery for transferring powers to the king and parliament, but the king was seen as an Ottoman holdover, and the parliament served only the rich landowning and professional classes, which the British dominated. In most matters crucial to Egyptians, Britain did not even pretend to yield. It refused to give up control of the Suez Canal, Egypt's army, or Britain's military bases. It made clear it would run Egypt's foreign policy. It retained the economic privileges it had long before extracted, including the immunity from local law of the foreigners who, under old "capitulations" treaties, ran Egypt's business affairs. Britain also insisted on Egypt's renunciation of its claim to the Sudan, which London intended to govern.

Significantly, accepting Britain's concept of independence would have given Egypt less power than it would have had under a mandate. As a mandate, if Egypt wanted to challenge Britain, it had recourse at least in theory to the League of Nations. Not fooled by Britain's make-believe, Egyptians simply refused to acknowledge the offer.

"Democracy," Mahfouz told me when we talked in Cairo some years ago, explaining what had happened in Egypt then and since, "is not deeply rooted in our culture. The people would make sacrifices for independence but not for democracy, and so step by step our system fell apart. The generation that came after mine blamed democracy for the corruption of the monarchy and for the privileges of the rich. I believe the blame belongs to Britain's colonialism. But whoever was responsible, when we tried it in the years after 1919, most Egyptians concluded that it offered nothing—not social justice, not freedom, not even full independence. They laughed at democracy."

Nearly four decades more of angry confrontation and sporadic violence would pass before Egyptian independence became a reality. The conflict fueled the fury of Arab nationalism, breeding hatred throughout the region. By the time independence came, whatever goodwill existed between Arabs and their colonial rulers had all but disappeared. As for parliamentary rule, whatever seeds were sown under the British failed to bloom; in fact, the blossoms of real democracy have yet to make an appearance in Egypt's political life.

—

Turkey, meanwhile, was taking a stand under Mustafa Kemal, the general who had beaten the Allied armies at Gallipoli. Born in 1880 in Salonika, a provincial city divided among Turks, Greeks, and Jews, Kemal attended secular schools before passing an exam to enter the military academy. The Ottoman army at that time was the most successful product of the empire's effort to impart Western reforms to its institutions. As a student, Kemal dabbled in popular protests seeking to Westernize the sultanate and was even jailed for a time. But he was too independent, even aloof, to join fellow officers in the Young Turk movement. In fact, he opposed joining the war in 1914, out of distaste for the Germans. Having performed brilliantly at Gallipoli, he went on to further victories against the Russians in the east, but his temperament alienated him from his contemporaries in the CUP, and he spent the last years of the war in idleness.

In 1920 the sultan's government, responding to its British

occupiers, sent Kemal to Ankara, a town in central Anatolia, to suppress the popular unrest in the region. The assignment placed him at a critical site. The Treaty of Sèvres had inflamed the memory of the Ottomans' long conflict with the West. Christian invaders—British and French, Greek and Italian, even the local Armenians—were taking deep bites out of Turkish territory. Turks perceived them all as infidels ravishing the Muslim patrimony. Though secular, Kemal shared this conception, and by the time he arrived in Ankara, local Turks were spontaneously organizing militias and guerrilla bands. Europe had failed to understand how inspired the Turkish masses, emerging from the demoralization of a lost war, could be in defending their homeland.

Kemal—who would later be called Ataturk, "Father Turk"—proved to be a skilled leader not only in battle but in politics. He hammered the makeshift military units into a redoubtable army; more important, he began the transformation of the Turkish masses from fallen-away Ottomans to present-day Turkish nationalists. His victories on the battlefield inspired the Arabs, in turn, by showing that being Muslim was an index not of weakness but of strength in taking on the Christian powers. Ataturk demolished the Treaty of Sèvres and created a Turkish nation, imparting to Arabs the lesson that they, too, could take charge of their fate.

Under Kemal, the sequence began with the Italians, whom the Allies late in the war had cajoled into joining them with a secret promise of territorial spoils in Anatolia. In 1919, on their own, the Italians set up a beachhead on Turkey's Mediterranean coast. The British, furious at Italy's presumption in not consulting them, convinced Wilson that the attack violated self-determination. The American president, after briefly considering deployment of U.S. forces, authorized the Greeks to dislodge the Italians. The presence of Greece, covetous of its ancient dominion in Anatolia, filled the Turks with a sense of national jeopardy.

The Greek invasion gave definition to Kemal's mission. From his Anatolian base, he proclaimed a national pact, in which he vowed to turn back all foreign intruders. His first major victory, over the French dug into positions on Syria's border, persuaded Paris that to subdue renascent Turkey was not worth the cost. Italy soon reached the same conclusion. Britain, however, was unyielding. Relying on its army in Constantinople, it dismissed Turkey's parliament, arrested hundreds of officials, and forced the sultan to denounce Kemal's resistance. The sultanate's submission stripped it of its last fragment of national credibility.

Kemal proceeded to bring together leaders from all Anatolia, forming in Ankara the Grand National Assembly, a renegade parliament, free from British power, which became the foundation of the new Turkish state. When Britain recruited an army composed of Kurds and pro-sultanate Turks, Kemal's forces crushed it. Then he went on the offensive against the Greeks, beating them badly in July 1921, and even worse a year later. His final triumph drove the remnants of Greece's army back to their homeland. Kemal had by then swept out of Anatolia all the intruders who had arrived under the mantle of the Treaty of Sèvres.

With Turkey again a power, Kemal negotiated accords with France and Italy that shredded the Treaty of Sèvres. He also reached an agreement restoring relations with Bolshevik Russia. Bringing around Britain and Greece, who still occupied European Turkey, took longer, but the British lacked the resources to persevere. "We are negotiating now with an enemy who has an army in being while we have none," said Lord Curzon, the foreign secretary. In September 1922, Britain repatriated the last of Greece's forces and two months later agreed to withdraw its own army from Constantinople and the Bosporus. Britain also agreed to drop the references in the Treaty of Sèvres to Kurdish or Armenian states.

Britain's withdrawal left the sultan, the final vestige of Ottoman rule, without support. Backed by the Grand National Assembly, Kemal proceeded to abolish the office, sending its last sultan into exile. Within a few years, he would also abolish the parallel office of the caliphate, solidifying Turkey's identity as a secular state. Kemal's subsequent reforms launched Turkey on a course of Westernization from which it has sometimes wavered but never turned back. His place in history is marked not just by national liberation but by social revolution.

The Arabs, awed as they were by Turkey's liberation, were cool to the aspect of social revolution. Arabs have been noticeably uncomfortable with Turkey's road to modernity, especially the challenge to Islam perceived in Kemal's secular ways. Though some Arab states have adopted secular practices, notably with regard to women, none has emulated Turkey's fundamental transformation. Many Arabs, in fact, condemn what Kemal did as apostasy.

Kemal's victory over the combined forces of the West in 1921 and 1922 no doubt provided the Turks with a psychological dynamism that eased the process of Westernization. The Arabs' consistent failure to achieve comparable victories on the battlefield generated a contrary dynamic, uniting them around their familiar values, and increasingly around their religion. Though Turkish and Arab nationalism have roots in common, in the decades after World War I, the Turks' distrust of the West has softened, while the animosity of the Arabs has intensified. These trends pervade the two societies today.

———

After the Treaty of Sèvres, France began mobilizing its army to realize the mandate for Syria that it had acquired. In legitimizing France's claim, the signers at Sèvres abrogated Faisal's. It was a decision the Arabs could not accept. In the ensuing months, Faisal's guerrillas sporadically attacked the French army that was organizing in Lebanon, while Arab irregulars collaborated with Kemal's forces against the French units on Syria's border. By mid-1920, however, France's buildup was sufficient for it to take the offensive.

On July 14, the French army commander sent Faisal an ultimatum laying out demands based on the prerogatives set out at Sèvres. Faisal, surprisingly, announced his willingness to accept them. Throughout Syria, protests erupted against Faisal's submission, most violently in Aleppo, where townspeople joined Bedouins from the desert in a rampage through the city. The insurgency stiffened Faisal's resistance, but the French military command was not deterred.

Headed inland, France's main force was met by a ragtag Syrian army, composed largely of poorly trained volunteers, at the village of Maysalun on the Damascus road. The commander of the volunteers was an ex-Ottoman officer who had joined Sharif Hussein in 1916; proclaiming that honor was at stake, he died in fierce fighting on the battlefield. Despite its defeat, the bravery of the defenders made Maysalun a Syrian legend. A day after their victory, the French entered Damascus and, in an effort to break their spirit, imposed a heavy indemnity on the inhabitants. In the ensuing weeks, the French occupied all of Syria's cities and towns and much of the countryside.

The French military administration resolved the problem of Faisal's presence by ordering him into exile. On July 28, 1920, the man who had captured Damascus reversed the route his forces had taken and left the country. After a stop in Italy, he accepted a British offer to settle in London. Britain, though disapproving of France's shabby treatment of Faisal, accepted no blame for its own complicity. In inviting him to

London, however, Britain recognized that Faisal's services might again be valuable to them.

Adopting a divide-and-conquer policy, the French wasted no time in putting their stamp on Syria. They decreed autonomous states for the deviant Muslim sects, Alawites and Druzes, as well as for the city of Aleppo, effectively isolating troublesome Damascus. They also formalized Lebanon's status as a separate state within the mandate, confirming the Maronite Christians as the dominant force. To enhance Maronite power further, they widened Lebanon's boundaries to include sectors with preponderantly Muslim populations. Over time this move backfired by diluting the Maronites' majority, leading in the 1970s to a horrible civil war. But to the French in 1920, their segmentation of Syria appeared a shrewd way to ensure their supremacy.

Still, the Syrian population was restless. France imposed martial law, to little effect. Though its practices violated the responsibilities of a mandatory power as stated in the League of Nations charter, the League proved an impotent body. Under the provocation of the French, Syria's nationalism, once shallow and fragmented, grew pervasive and deep. Within a few years, it was ready to explode.

The explosion was ignited by the Druzes in 1925, when a French aircraft was shot down and the crew of a French rescue mission was ambushed, leaving one hundred dead. The incident sparked an insurgency that spread across the country. Its leaders coordinated their actions. The Druzes alone quietly placed several thousand disciplined men under arms. In morale the Syrians surpassed the French, whose army was now composed largely of poorly motivated colonials who were loath to fight.

The insurgency—called by Syrians the Great Revolt—drew support from Arabs everywhere. Despite French reinforcements, fierce fighting went on for two years, at a cost of ruined cities and thousands of lives. Though France won the war, the price was huge. The revolt became a watershed for Arab nationalism, elevating popular fervor; in the end, European colonialism could not defeat it.

France proposed a settlement of the insurgency in 1927, but its terms were reminiscent of Britain's hollow offer to Egypt in 1922. France offered Syria the façade of independence without the substance. Nothing came of it, and in 1928 France organized an election, which produced a Syrian parliament as radical as the one that had greeted Faisal in 1920. The majority, calling itself the National Bloc, demanded a unified Syria, to include not just the Alawite, Druze, and Aleppo regions but Lebanon and Palestine as well. The bloc also demanded Syrian control over the army and foreign affairs. France's response was to send the parliament home.

The dissolution produced another year of violence, with strikes and rioting almost daily. France offered a plan of independence without the limits it had insisted on earlier, but the proposal was to apply only to a truncated Syria, consisting of Aleppo and Damascus, leaving the other regions, notably Lebanon, under French control. When the offer failed to break the deadlock, the French held a new election, and despite the pains they took to rig it, the new majority was no more accommodating. France then dissolved the parliament again.

The hostility simmered until 1936, when a massive general strike combined with the installation of a more liberal government in France to break the deadlock. A Syrian delegation was invited to Paris, and in return for independence, it reluctantly conceded the loss of Lebanon and Palestine. The two sides then signed an accord. The delegation returned from Paris to a rapturous welcome, and after an election in late 1936, the nationalist majority ratified the treaty.

But the treaty never went into effect. In another cabinet shift, France's colonial partisans regained power. Moreover, war with Germany was again looming, and the colonial lobby was clamoring that the treaty with Syria would pass the germ of independence on to France's North African possessions, putting its Mediterranean defenses in jeopardy. In the context of the turmoil rising in Europe, the treaty died, and Syria's angry nationalists decided, at least for the time being, to forgo further conflict.[6]

———

Iraq entered the post–World War I era without the hard-core nationalism that now pervaded Syria. Iraqis, to be sure, shared with other Arabs the historical memory of conflict with the Christian West. But, in having stood with the Ottomans against the British invasion, they were slow to embrace a new Arab identity. Iraqi soldiers who defected to the Arab army after 1917 tended to vow their allegiance to Faisal personally, not to an Arab nation. Yet, shallow as their nationalism was, Iraqis resolved after the war that Britain would not replace the Ottoman Empire. Iraq, too, demanded independence.

Iraqi nationalism faced major obstacles, however. The state created by the Treaty of Sèvres was far from organic. Historic Mesopotamia was composed of rival Shi'ites, Sunnis, and Kurds; Christians, Turkmen, and Jews; peasants, bourgeoisie, and Bedouins. It had always been a fractious mix. Statehood by no means swept away its differences. It was Britain's imperious rule after the Treaty of Sèvres that provided Iraqis with a common national cause.

Iraqis, many still armed when the fighting stopped, erupted after the announcement that Britain had been awarded the Iraq mandate. The Iraqis who had harassed the British during the war stepped up their attacks on Britain's occupation forces, using the hit-and-run tactics at which Arabs excelled. A fierce insurgency cut off towns and cities, bombed trains and military installations. Though the British were as ruthless as the French at suppression, the fighting cost them hundreds of lives, plus monetary expenditures that London could ill afford. The costs made the British amenable to a political settlement, the key to which they saw in the person of Prince Faisal, the deposed king of Syria, now sitting idle in London.

In July 1921, the British declared Faisal the king of Iraq. The provisional government that Britain named obediently approved the choice, which was then ratified in a plebiscite. To burnish the appearance of legitimacy, the British crafted a treaty and the kind of constitution that they and the French were trying to sell throughout the region. They offered Iraq a smattering of independence but reserved for themselves authority over vital security matters. The constitution provided for a British high commissioner to watch over a largely powerless king and parliament. The Iraqis were not fooled by the deal any more than had been the Egyptians or Syrians.

Faisal had many problems in addition to the British. Iraqis, in their diversity, had serious reservations about one another: Kurds, yearning for their own independence, resented Arab domination; Shi'ites, by far the numerical majority, resented the Sunni preeminence. To govern, Faisal relied heavily on ex-Ottoman officers who had served in his army, almost all Sunni. Most notable among them was Nuri Said, who had been among the first to give his allegiance to the Arab Revolt. These men held most of the high offices and established surprisingly efficient administrative and educational systems. Nuri himself founded an army—which, decades later, would turn viciously against him. In time Faisal, as a dedicated king, succeeded in winning the hearts of most Iraqis. Yet neither he nor his monarchy ever quite overcame the taint of being the offspring of British power.

Faisal helped to win the parliament's approval of the constitution Britain had proposed. He also endorsed a treaty with the British that gave Iraq a seat in the League of Nations. Iraq under Faisal was far less violent than Syria under the French, and in 1932 the British theoretically ended the mandate and withdrew some of their forces. But with Iraqi nationalism still growing, few Iraqis showed real confidence in their governing institutions, which they continued to see as instruments of colonial rule.

Early in the 1930s, Iraq's army emerged as a political force, and when Faisal died in 1933, his son Ghazi, the successor to his throne, proved much less able than his father to contain it. Nationalist officers flirted with the authoritarian ideology rising in Europe and, in 1936, attempted the first of a series of armed coups. The parliamentary regime survived through trade-offs in favors among political and military factions. But, poorly designed as it was for promoting the country's interests, the process advanced the army's claim to be the champion of Iraqi nationalism against Britain and the monarchy.

Britain's image was also tainted by events outside Iraq. In 1936, the year of the first coup, the British aroused popular ire by suppressing a revolt of the Arabs of Palestine. Hajj Amin al-Husseini, the Palestinian leader, succeeded in taking refuge in Baghdad, adding his voice to the anti-British clamor.

Hardly had World War II begun than another crisis loomed when a cabal of the army's most fiercely nationalist officers took command. In March 1941, Rashid Ali al-Kaylani, a politician beholden to the military cabal, formed a pro-German cabinet, jeopardizing Britain's positions throughout the region. King Ghazi's death in a road accident in 1939 had left his uncle Prince Abd al-Ilah as the regent in charge. The cabinet proceeded to repudiate an agreement requiring Iraq to come to Britain's support in case of war, provoking the British to demand Rashid Ali's removal. Abd al-Ilah sided with Britain, but the army was loyal to its officers, forcing him to take flight aboard a British warship. Britain then dispatched Jordan's Arab Legion to occupy Iraq.

In what Iraqis call the Second British Occupation, Britain

restored the power of Abd al-Ilah, who reconstituted an Iraqi government made up of supporters of Britain. He also exacted harsh retribution against opponents of the monarchy. Though Rashid Ali himself escaped, along with Hajj Amin, the army officers behind the coup were captured and executed. Hundreds of Rashid Ali sympathizers, in addition, were interned in British prison camps. With the approval of the Abd al-Ilah regime, the Iraqi constitution was amended to make sure that such loss of control to anti-British elements would not be repeated.

Whatever Britain's justification in time of war, the result of the countercoup was to blur in the eyes of the Iraqi public the distinction between the monarchy and the occupier. Abd al-Ilah, in embracing Britain's interests, hammered still another nail into the coffin of Iraq's constitutional monarchy. Irate and sullen, the remnants of the Iraqi army became more extreme in their nationalism and began preparing to counterattack.

———

In 1922 the Council of the League of Nations, in conveying the Palestine mandate to Britain, held it "responsible for putting into effect" the Balfour Declaration, which promised a "national home" to the Jewish people. This unusual provision emerged, said the document, from "the historical connection of the Jewish people with Palestine." The mandatory text pledged to facilitate Jewish immigration and to develop self-governing institutions. It also imparted special powers to "the Zionist organization" to assist in the establishment of the Jewish national home.

The mandatory document makes no comparable vows to the Arabs of Palestine, who at the time composed 90 percent of the population. Nowhere, in fact, does it mention "Arab" or "Palestinian" at all. The text refers to the Arabs as "existing non-Jewish communities" and pledges to safeguard their "civil and religious rights." It provides a concession in naming Arabic an official language, requiring that it be used, along with Hebrew and English, on stamps and currency. But it says nothing of political rights, much less any right of self-determination. It is not surprising that Arabs everywhere perceived the mandate as discriminatory, placing the Palestinian Arabs in a position much inferior to the Jews.[7]

When the mandate started, nationalism among Palestinians, as among most other Arabs, was still in a nascent state. But, as the mandatory text made clear, Palestine differed from Britain's other Middle East acquisitions, where the Arabs confronted colonial power directly. In Palestine, the Arabs confronted the Jews. Britain's role was never quite clear, not even to itself. Though Britain took seriously its vows under the Balfour Declaration, at times it bestowed favors on the Arabs and at other times it played—poorly, for the most part—the intermediary between the two communities. In the end, satisfying neither, Britain left Palestine, loathed by Arabs and Jews alike.

British personnel serving in Palestine understood the dilemma much more clearly than did the policy establishment in London. Their reservations about British policy were not necessarily anti-Zionist, much less anti-Semitic, though they were accused, sometimes justly, of both. What they perceived was that Arab and Jewish interests were irreconcilable, and that Britain would inevitably be ground down between them. Throughout 1919, while the world awaited the outcome of the Paris peace conference and tensions rose, both Arabs and Jews held their fire. But the calm was deceptive, and by early 1920 the Palestine powder keg was ready to explode.

The British, who had never shown much skill in dealing with any nationalism, were particularly vexed that in Palestine they had to face not one nationalism but two. The contrast between Jewish and Arab nationalism, moreover, was considerable. The Jews, most of them Europeans with skills in diplomacy, economics, and the arts, were also adept at organizing themselves. The Arabs, though numerically superior, were in organizational disarray. After four centuries of Turkish rule, they had no trained leaders; neither had they a political strategy or a grasp of bargaining strategy. Their nationalism, fueled by righteous rage, had an all-or-nothing quality, sparking eruptions that wasted blood and resources.

Historians say the killing began at Tel Hai, a small colony in the Galilee, where Jews, living amid Arab villages, tilled the land. Animosity between the communities, once minimal, escalated as Palestinians came to perceive from the Balfour Declaration that Jewish numbers placed their own society in jeopardy. Only a few hours away by road, Syria was aflame with resistance to the French, exacerbating the anger.

In March 1920, a chance encounter between farmers outside Tel Hai ignited a firefight, to which Jews rushed reinforcements. The Jewish leader was Josef Trumpeldor, a zealous Zionist who, as an officer in the czar's army, had been a hero of the Russo-Japanese war. Trumpeldor was among the five Arabs and five Jews killed in the skirmish. With both sides exalting the martyrdom of their victims, Tel Hai imparted fresh legitimacy to armed conflict.

In the Old City of Jerusalem on the following Easter weekend, during the Muslim feast of Nebi Musa, a more serious explosion occurred. The Nebi Musa celebration was traditionally disorderly. The Turks had policed it tightly, but the British, despite signs of restlessness, deployed only a skeleton force as a deterrent. Some fifty thousand Arabs with a political agenda jammed the Old City's narrow streets, shouting, "Independence! Independence!"

Witnesses generally agree that the Arabs initiated the violence, directing much of it at Jewish families, whose residence in the Old City long predated Zionism. Homes were looted and vandalized, pedestrians beaten and stabbed. Though the British imposed martial law, the disorders raged for four days, leaving five Jews and three Arabs dead. Seeking evenhandedness, the British authorities brought some two hundred participants, both Jews and Arabs, to trial, with the result that both felt misused. Soon, however, the losses on Nebi Musa would seem trivial. A year later rioting that began in Jaffa spread through all of Palestine, leaving a hundred dead. The intensity of the Arab-Jewish conflict was now soaring.[8]

For a moment it appeared the Arabs had discovered in violence a viable weapon to achieve their political end. Sir Herbert Samuel, Britain's high commissioner, was obviously intimidated by it. Samuel, a Zionist and a Jew himself, had been appointed to implement the Balfour Declaration, but, as a conscientious civil servant, he sent London a recommendation to limit Jewish immigration and elect a consultative assembly, which he knew the Arabs would dominate. The Arabs, however, were not satisfied and demanded not just Balfour's recision but cancellation of the mandate itself. The Jews, whatever their indignation, breathed a sigh of relief as the Arabs made diplomatic intransigence the companion of their violence. Principled though the Arabs may have been, the rejection of any compromise arrangement with the Jews led them down a blind alley, from which they have not yet exited.

In Hajj Amin al-Husseini, the Arabs possessed a leader who, though initially disinclined to violence, left no doubt about his loathing for the Balfour Declaration. The British, to resolve a local factional rivalry, had arranged in 1921 to have him named mufti of Jerusalem, then expanded the jurisdiction of his office to make him the spiritual leader of Muslims in all Palestine. A year later Britain formed the Supreme Muslim Council, a quasi parliament, which he headed, adding administrative authority. Still later, in emulation of the local Jews, Arab leaders founded the Arab Higher Committee, which gave Hajj Amin still another office, and by the mid-1920s he led the Palestinian Arabs in both politics and religion.

For most of that decade, Hajj Amin intruded little into the worsening communal relations. But, in 1929 he endorsed a popular protest against Jewish worship at the Wailing Wall, and before it was over, hundreds were dead.

The rise of Hitler aggravated the problem, with Jews by the thousands seeking refuge in Palestine. The Arabs feared, with some justification, that they would soon be overwhelmed. In 1936 Hajj Amin, demanding restrictions on Jewish immigration and land transfers, became the leader of a full-scale revolt, directed against both Jews and the British. After a thousand Arabs died, most of them at the hands of British forces, he called a truce, in return for which Britain agreed to name a royal commission to seek an equitable settlement. Both Hajj Amin and the Zionists testified before what was known as the Peel Commission, while the revolt simmered in anticipation of its recommendations.

The commission's report, delivered in 1937, stunned all sides in proposing that Palestine be divided between self-governing Arab and Jewish entities. While it urged a population transfer to assure homogeneity within each sector, along with the establishment of a British enclave in Jerusalem, the main contribution of the Peel Commission was to place the concept of "partition" at the center of the Palestine debate. It has remained there since.

London accepted the Peel report at once. But Jews and Arabs, both faithful to the principle of an undivided Palestine—which each expected to rule—were not enthusiastic. Partition was a new idea. Even today it generates dispute. The Zionists, split over the prospect of a truncated state, gave no clear answer to the recommendation. Hajj Amin and the Arabs, however, barely deliberated. To the Jews' relief, they took the responsibility for scuttling the Peel report, rejecting partition flatly.

The revolt in Palestine resumed in greater force in September 1937, after Arabs assassinated a British police commissioner in Nazareth. Not only did Palestinians fight but thousands of Arab volunteers rallied from outside Palestine. That is when Hajj Amin fled to Baghdad, but he continued to direct his followers from hiding. Jews, meanwhile, took to the field with organized units that they had for years been training in secret. Britain brought in reinforcements of men, armor, and aircraft. By the best estimate, before the conflict sputtered to an end on the eve of the new world war, it had cost the lives of three thousand Arabs, two thousand Jews, and six hundred Britons.

Yet the revolt settled nothing. The looming European war imposed a temporary calm on Palestine, but it was clearly temporary. Britain, preoccupied with the Axis and unwilling to provoke the Arab world, retreated from the Peel recommendations. In fact, it retreated from the Balfour Declaration itself. But the last word had not been said. Few doubted that the Arab-Jewish struggle would resume as soon as the European war was over.

———

On the other side of the Jordan River, the British followed a much different course. Known as Transjordan, the land was largely desert, populated by Bedouin tribes. The League of Nations had placed it within the Palestine mandate, which gave some Zionists reason to claim it under the Balfour Declaration. Militant Zionists, in fact, long called for a homeland on "both sides of the Jordan." But Transjordan was not considered part of historic Palestine, and Britain had been prudent enough to include in the mandatory texts the authority to treat it separately. Furthermore, under the Sykes-Picot Agreement, otherwise so ungenerous to the Arabs, the Transjordan region was recognized as Arab territory, probably because neither Britain nor France thought it was worth the trouble to govern.

In the 1920s, however, Britain perceived Transjordan's virtues as a buffer between Palestine and the irascible French in Syria, as well as the aggressive Sauds to the south. They also saw it as a corridor between the Mediterranean and the Gulf, a land route to their possessions farther east. Barren as it was, they acquired a resolve not to give it up. Lacking resources, however, they faced a dilemma over how to hold it.

In 1921 London came up with a remedy, not unlike its solution in Iraq. It invited Abdullah, older brother of King Faisal, to rule Transjordan. Abdullah's talents were regarded as more modest than Faisal's. He had a reputation for indolence. When he was a military commander, he had failed dismally in his one major test, a battle against the Sauds. Yet the British were sensitive to Sharif Hussein's charge that they had betrayed him and saw the offer to Abdullah as a partial recompense. Their only requirement, which seemed little enough to ask, was that Abdullah keep Transjordan's Bedouins from adding to their woes by provoking the French, the Wahhabis, and the Zionists, who lived nearby.

Abdullah, however, had ideas of his own. Like his father, he thought of his family, the Hashemites, as destined to rule a great Arab state. In this framework, Britain's offer of Transjordan seemed stingy, and he agreed only tentatively to accept it. In the ensuing months, France complained of provocations in Syria that seemed to confirm Abdullah's grand designs. The Sauds also protested his promotion of Hashemite interests in Arabia. Abdullah, however, liked his new throne and, under pressure from Britain, backed away from the demands for Arab statehood. This retreat persuaded Britain that he would not be an obstacle to their own strategic control of the territory.

The British bestowed on Abdullah the title *emir*, "prince," along with a substantial annual subsidy. The quid pro quo for Britain, laid out in a treaty that described Transjordan as independent, was military bases, as well as the services of Abdullah's army. Jordan's forces, later celebrated as the Arab Legion, helped quell the Palestinian uprising in 1939 and the Rashid Ali rebellion in Iraq two years later. In the Arab world, Abdullah's willingness to use his army against other Arabs constituted proof of his capitulation to Western colonialism and his betrayal of Arab nationalism. This perception would undermine his status and that of his heirs for generations to come.

Through the turmoil, Abdullah maintained his close ties with his father, still ruler in the Hejaz. Abdullah helped him in the conflict with the House of Saud, which by now had spilled out of Arabia. In 1922 the Sauds sent thousands of Wahhabi warriors mounted on camels into Transjordan to bring Abdullah down. Only British airplanes and armored cars saved the monarchy.

Two years later the Sauds changed direction and launched an attack on the Hejaz directly. Hussein, who now called himself king, had steadily lost ground in Arabia since World War I ended in 1918. Much of the loss was his own doing. He was widely disliked by his subjects for tolerating corruption. He was incompetent in administration and politics. Arabia's tribesmen, little interested in the wider world, forgot his role in the Arab Revolt. When the Sauds attacked the Hejaz in 1924, the British, who now looked on Hussein's cause as hopeless, decided to ignore his pleas for help. Alone, Sharif Hussein was no match for the Wahhabi power under Saudi command.

Fearful of Wahhabi conquest, Hussein's subjects called for

him to abdicate as the enemy neared. In October 1924 the sharif surrendered the throne to his eldest son, Ali. He stubbornly resisted exile, however, and only under pressure from the tribes left for Amman, Abdullah's capital. Yet he remained steadfast in believing his destiny was to rule the Arab nation. In departing, he issued what he called "my final protest," lamenting that his abdication "will lead to the fragmentation of the Arabs and the loss of their essential rights."

In Amman, Sharif Hussein continued to behave like a king, receiving Arab delegations that indulged him with empty assurances of their loyalty. Clearly convinced he was a more rightful ruler than his son, he quarreled constantly with Abdullah. Hussein was in Amman when the news arrived that Mustafa Kemal had abolished the caliphate, and he promptly declared that, yielding to pleas from Muslims everywhere, he would accept the office. No one paid attention. At that point, Abdullah withdrew his welcome to his father, and Hussein left Amman for Aqaba, the site where the Arab Revolt had won its first great victory.

But he could not stay there, either. He was shadowed by the Sauds, who coveted Aqaba as a port and took his presence there as a pretext to seize it. But for the British, Aqaba was a link in their own regional designs. It served them as a doorway to the Arab hinterland and to the Suez Canal. Britain sent its own military units, which stopped the Saud advance. Then, showing its confidence in Abdullah's reliability, Britain announced the transfer of Aqaba and the region around it from Hejazi to Transjordanian sovereignty. That is where it remains to this day.

But Britain made no effort to halt the Saud conquest of the Hejaz. Mecca fell to the Sauds in October 1925, and Medina in December, after which Ali, Hussein's son, went into exile in Iraq. His departure united virtually all of Arabia under the House of Saud, a huge victory for Wahhabi puritanism. The victory, ending more than a millennium of Hashemite dominion in the peninsula, closed the curtain ignominiously on Sharif Hussein's grand design for Arab nationhood.

Hussein's final years were melancholy, even pitiful. When the British insisted he leave Aqaba, no Arab state would have him. So Britain put him aboard a warship headed for Cyprus. In departing, Hussein looked back on the ties first established with McMahon in 1915 and declared sadly, "I have been truly loyal to the British, trusting that the government would maintain its policies and those agreements which it made with regard to Arab rights, Arab unity and the freedom of those Arabs who fought as its allies." He exaggerated little, if at all, in concluding, "We have kept strictly to our side of the agreement."

In Cyprus, Hussein was a solitary figure. Few of his companions there were Arabs or even spoke Arabic. His only regular company was his youngest son, Zaid. Finally, at age seventy-nine and paralyzed with a stroke, he received permission from Abdullah to return to Amman. He died there in 1931, all but forgotten as the leader of the Arab Revolt and the father of modern Arab nationalism.

In retrospect, it is clear Hussein was in many ways a misfit. In later years, he suffered from delusions and may even have been mentally disturbed. But had he been a conventional Arab ruler, cautious in his calculations and deferential to established authority, there would have been no Arab Revolt. Without it, there would have been no Arab struggle for independence, much less Arab grandeur. Hussein's audacity, for better or worse, restored the Arabs to a place of their own in history.

Some critics regard the Arab Revolt as a dismal failure. Some Arabs still deny that Hussein had a right to abandon the Ottomans and Islam for an alliance with the Christian West.

But whatever its failings, the revolt was a heroic undertaking, and thanks to the alliance with the Christian West, the Arabs broke with centuries of international invisibility. Without the Arab Revolt, the Arabs, in the years that ensued, would have lived their collective life on a lesser, more mundane plane. Hussein sparked a transformation of the Arab world that was irreversible. His shortcomings as a leader were many, but he remains a transcendent figure in the history of the Arab people.

Consistent with the tragedy of his life, Hussein, at his funeral in Jerusalem in 1931, was ignored by the Arabs. His coffin was escorted by a guard of honor of British soldiers.[9]

IV

EMANCIPATION

1940-1956

In the period between the World Wars, Europe's colonial governments in the Middle East successfully preserved their hegemony over their Arab possessions. Having made a mockery of President Wilson's promises of self-determination, they suppressed resistance brutally, keeping tight controls beneath a façade of democracy. But successful as they were, under the surface their policies ignited rising fires of nationalist emotions.

This nationalism was essentially secular. Though Islam was an integral part of the concept of Arab nationhood, Sharif Hussein had failed to convince Arabs that *his* Islam was more legitimate than the Ottomans'. Few Arabs shared his interest in restoring an Arab caliphate, and fewer still sympathized with his aspiration to hold the office himself. Whatever the religious component of the Arab Revolt, its goal of independence made it essentially a political struggle. After the war, the new Arab regimes shaped their own ongoing fight for independence in secular terms.

It is not that Arab nationalism was ever antireligious. As long as the Ottomans held power, the Islamic establishment of the Arab community, conservative by nature, was loath to embrace the idea of Arab independence. Sharif Hussein's identification of Arab nationalism with the Christian West kept it further at bay. In the Arab Revolt, the Islamic clergy were clearly on the Ottoman side. Yet, unlike much of Europe's nationalism, Arab nationalism, when it emerged as a powerful force, did not regard clericalism as an enemy.

Whatever breach existed between Arab nationalism and

Islam narrowed after the fall of the Ottomans left the clergy adrift. Mustafa Kemal's abolishment of the caliphate intensified the clergy's sense of isolation. By the 1920s, however, the Christian West, its imperialism full blown, had resumed its historic role as the Arabs' enemy. Comfortable as a fortress against the infidels, the Islamic establishment enlisted in the struggle for Arab independence.

It was not long before Islamic doctrine drifted into the void left by the caliphate's liquidation, creating a religious nationalism to compete with secular nationalism for the Arabs' allegiance. Since its inception, religious nationalism has proven an inextinguishable force in the Arab world.

The roots of religious nationalism can be dated to the years immediately after the caliphate disappeared. In 1928 Hassan al-Banna founded the Muslim Brotherhood. Al-Banna, born into a religious family in the Nile Delta in 1906, attended Islamic primary schools, then went off to Cairo at the age of sixteen to study Islamic law. Egypt at the time was throbbing with anticolonial feeling. Fiercely committed to Egypt's independence, al-Banna was unhappy with the secular framework in which the fight was being conducted. Though he soon abandoned his plan for the caliphate's restoration, he vowed to reshape Arab nationalism, along with Arab society itself, within the framework of Islam.

When he founded the brotherhood, al-Banna was a teacher living among the Egyptian laborers who performed the maintenance work on the Suez Canal. Appalled by the conditions in which they lived, he sought to offer them better lives. Al-Banna did not see secular nationalism as his ally. "The point of contention between us and them," he once said, "is that we define patriotism in terms of creed . . . not territorial boundaries. Every region in which there is a Muslim . . . is a homeland for us." Deeply committed as he was to political emancipation, it

was not enough. Al-Banna linked independence and social reform to a return of the Arabs to the rigorous practice of Islam.

Al-Banna's record leaves no doubt that he was brilliant as
both proselytizer and organizer. That he attracted the poor by
promoting social services is understandable. But he also gathered recruits from the middle classes, an audience unmoored
by Islam's post-Ottoman transformation. When al-Banna relocated from the delta to Cairo in 1932, the brotherhood's
Egyptian members already numbered in the tens of thousands. A few years later, his efforts beyond Egypt's borders
yielded a membership in the millions, with branches in every
Arab country.

Al-Banna's vision was liberation of the *umma* from foreign
rule and the establishment, in its place, of a state of all Muslims, governed by the *shari'a*. His teaching went beyond politics, however, to spiritual reawakening. He envisaged the
allegiance of the Arabs to a rigorous Islamic puritanism, from
which the corrupting ideas of the West would be perma-
nently extruded.

Still, al-Banna had to start in Egypt, from which banishing
the British was the sine qua non of his program. Convinced the
British would not leave peacefully, he laid the groundwork for
violence by contending that Islam enjoined whatever means
were needed to achieve its holy goals. Designating himself
the Supreme Guide, he was careful not to call publicly for
bloodshed, but his clear tilt toward *jihad* led the brotherhood
to organize a "secret apparatus." By the eve of World War II,
the brotherhood's assassins were targeting not just British officials but Egyptian collaborators.

When the war began and the Egyptian regime decided
to cooperate with Britain, the brotherhood went into fiercer
rebellion. Though not pro-Axis, al-Banna proclaimed publicly the need to replace the monarchy with an Islamic state.

The brotherhood's campaign, which simmered through the years of World War II, reached a climax in 1948, in the conflict between Arabs and Jews in Palestine. Al-Banna promoted Egypt's entry into the struggle and organized brotherhood contingents to fight. Meanwhile, the "secret apparatus" stepped up the spectacular assaults on public officials at home, culminating in the murder of the prime minister. The violence brought Egypt to the edge of anarchy. Six weeks after the prime minister's assassination, al-Banna was himself murdered, presumably in retaliation by the police. But the extremism he had sired was by now so deeply rooted that it no longer needed him to thrive.[1]

———

With the Allies victorious in World War II, but with colonial rule still firmly in place, many Arabs were ready to accept the Muslim Brotherhood's argument that the times demanded nothing less than violence. Had not the Arabs been assured, as they had been during Arab Revolt a generation earlier, that the war would end tyranny and bring them their freedom? In 1945, however, the Allies did even less to realize this goal than they had in 1919. They held no peace conference based on high ideals, and, though they founded the United Nations, they imbued it with no Wilsonian ideals. The Arabs sensed that the great empires were in retreat but that their own liberation would come only if they spilled blood to achieve it.

Events confirmed this analysis. Britain and France had not reconciled themselves to colonialism's demise. At best, they made small concessions, untidily, in niggling bargaining, while chaos dominated the Arab streets. They failed to grasp that, in barely more than a generation, their own practices had transformed the red coals of Arab nationalism into an inferno. Independence came to most Arabs after World War II, but painfully, producing a bitterness that has fed nationalist excesses to this day.

The fight for liberation began where it left off with the French in Syria. On the eve of World War II, France had reneged on the treaty of independence it had offered Syria and Lebanon. The French betrayed Syria further by ceding its northern port of Alexandretta to Turkey, in return for neutrality against the Axis. But France's strategy of saving itself by double-crossing the Arabs proved vain. In 1940 France was badly defeated in Europe and had to submit to the Nazi occupation of most of its territory. The French salvaged only a truncated state, with its capital in Vichy.

Under the armistice with the Nazis, the Vichy regime retained its control over Lebanon and Syria, and its terms required Vichy to grant the Germans no concessions. But in May 1941, Vichy submitted to the Nazi demand to refuel aircraft en route to support Rashid Ali's insurgency in Iraq. A month later, supplemented by General Charles de Gaulle's Free French, the British invaded Syria and, in heavy fighting, defeated Vichy's army.

That fall, the Free French, the nominal heirs to Vichy's rule, declared Syria and Lebanon independent, but the words were not matched by a transfer of power. In 1943 the Free French invited Syria and Lebanon to elect parliaments, and, in a repeat of the prewar vote, the two came under the dominance of ardent nationalists. Both the Syrian and the Lebanese parliaments created crises by voting to sever their ties with France.

Not surprisingly, the French rejected both declarations, and throughout 1944 the confrontation in Syria and Lebanon grew increasingly tense. In May 1945, as the war in Europe was ending, the French—as they had twenty-five years earlier—landed troops in Beirut as a prelude to reasserting their authority in the interior. Rioting broke out throughout the mandate, and a full-scale conflict seemed imminent. At that point, London delivered an ultimatum to the much weaker French to back off; resentfully, they did so. A month later France unexpectedly turned its Syrian mandate over to the United Nations and announced its withdrawal from the Middle East.

———

The British proved much more stubborn than the French. After Rashid Ali's uprising, they kept the lid on domestic unrest in Iraq by basing a substantial army there. The Iraqi monarchy, having defied popular will by siding with Britain during the uprising, took a further step in 1943 by joining Britain in declaring war on the Axis. Abd al-Ilah, the regent, and Nuri Said, his gray eminence, had consented to defer demands for full independence until the war was won, infuriating most Iraqis. But even Abd al-Ilah and Nuri expected the British to deliver on their vow when the fighting ended.

Yet when Iraq demanded repayment after the war for its patience, Britain stood firm. At the time of the Rashid Ali insurgency, the British had declared their reoccupation of Iraq to be temporary. Pointing to the treaty of independence they had dictated in 1930, they claimed that the mandate had been terminated long before. Whatever the faults of the 1930 treaty, Britain said, it had already granted Iraq as much freedom as it was prepared to concede.

The British recognized, of course, that even before World War II Iraqis had bristled at the limits of independence contained in the 1930 treaty. In empowering Britain not only to retain bases but to manage Iraq's foreign and defense policy, the treaty had in fact been the provocation for the Rashid Ali coup. Now Britain turned a deaf ear to the popular uproar which held that the monarchy existed only to do Britain's bidding. Finally, London offered to do some tinkering with the treaty, but Abd al-Ilah and Nuri understood that, with the nationalists demanding the abolition of the treaty in its entirety, any rewriting or tinkering with the old arrangement would not be enough. Both men understood, even if the British did not, that by now the throne itself was in jeopardy.

The confrontation was exacerbated by the rising Cold War between the West and Russia, as well as by the looming conflict between Arabs and Jews in Palestine. Abd al-Ilah argued that Britain's own self-interest demanded concessions, and for six months in 1948 the two sides actually bargained over their relationship at a naval base in Portsmouth, England. A new treaty was finally produced, with improved terms for Iraq, but it left both military installations and foreign policy in British hands. The Portsmouth Treaty was the last, best effort of the Hashemite regime, and when Iraqis learned of its contents, they took to the streets. Hundreds of Iraqis were dead before the rioting was over, and so was the revised treaty. The Iraqi monarchy never recovered.[2]

———

In contrast to Syria and Iraq, Transjordan remained on cordial terms with Britain, the product of its unique nature among the Arab states. Transjordan and the Hashemite regime that ruled it were pure British creations. Britain continued faithfully to deliver annual subsidies to Emir Abdullah. Transjordan's population seemed happy enough living its traditional tribal life. Transjordanians seemed to acknowledge that they needed Britain if their way of life was to survive.

By all measures, Transjordanians were proud of their ruler's pedigree as the Prophet's descendant. Unlike so many other Arab populations, they did not question the regime's legitimacy. It is true that Abdullah's roots, like those of the Iraqi kings, were in the Hejaz. But if he was an outsider, they did not consider him foreign. It was enough that, since Sharif Hussein's death, Abdullah was the senior member of the Hashemites, the Prophet's family.

Transjordan was also a country without nostalgia for Arab glory. It had no separate history; its entire past was linked to

Britain. Transjordanians had not made the leap to an awareness of membership in an Arab nation and, by all evidence,
were content to live within a familiar tribal framework. Unlike other Arabs, they nursed no dream of re-creating lost
grandeur. Their nationalist movement was tiny. Though Arab
nationalists outside their borders looked down on them,
Transjordanians did not seem to care. The kind of independence that was so important to Syrians and Iraqis was simply
not on their agenda.

Abdullah, to be sure, was sensitive to the disdain of other
Arabs, and, to satisfy him, Britain turned over more of the
trappings of sovereignty. It gave him the title of king and
granted him executive and legislative powers, though these
were limited by the British resident's authority. The limits
were basically the same as those Britain imposed on Iraq,
which Iraqis furiously rejected. But Transjordan did not dispute Britain's control over its armed forces, and over the
military bases Britain considered vital to its regional needs.
Because it trusted Transjordan, Britain ruled with a gentle
hand.

Yet Abdullah had never given up the Hashemite vision, his
father's dream, of ruling over a unified Arab nation. Back
in 1941, after the fighting that ended Vichy's rule of the
French mandate, he announced Transjordan's unification
with Lebanon and Syria to form a Hashemite Greater Syria.
Britain, anxious not to alienate its French allies, was incensed
and persuaded him to abandon the plan.

Then, in 1947, the United Nations resolution to partition
Palestine, heir of the prewar Peel proposal, presented Abdullah with what he saw as a new opportunity to advance the
Hashemite cause. Casting his eyes across the Jordan River,
he witnessed Arabs and Jews girding for war. Abdullah saw
the prospect of acquiring a major segment of territory there,

resuscitating his ambition to create a larger Arab nation under Hashemite rule.

———

As long as the outcome of World War II was in doubt, the Jews in Palestine had no alternative to supporting the British. In 1942 the military situation appeared particularly grim, with Axis divisions poised in Egypt's western desert, on the doorstep of the Middle East. Secretly, extremist Jews were mobilizing for terrorist warfare against Britain, while the Zionist leadership was organizing the Haganah as an army of liberation. But, with the Nazis nearby, both bided their time.

Then, in November 1942, Britain won a huge victory at El Alamein, putting the Germans to flight. El Alamein, in eliminating the Nazi threat to the Middle East, allowed the Zionists to go on the offensive.

The Zionists, like the Arabs, recognized that to obtain their independence they would have to fight Britain. The British had backtracked from the Balfour Declaration on the eve of World War II. They had also withdrawn their own proposal, the Peel report, for partitioning Palestine between Jews and Arabs. As the war went on, the Zionists had become increasingly persuaded that patience and diplomacy would not yield them the state they wanted. Far from seeking to appease the Jews, postwar Britain took a position that seemed almost irrationally hostile toward them.

In 1945, the year the war ended, the boiling issue was quotas for Jewish immigration from Europe to Palestine. Harry Truman, the new American president, entreated Britain to admit 100,000 of the 250,000 Jewish survivors of the Nazi concentration camps. Most were living in crowded refugee camps. With worldwide sympathy on the side of the Jews, Britain's refusal to admit them seemed inexcusably hardhearted.

Britain's naval blockade against Jewish refugees provoked a shift in Zionist policy. Until then, the Zionist leadership had kept the reins on the Haganah, its not-so-secret army. It had sought to discourage Zionist extremists, organized into rival factions, from the campaign of anti-British terrorism they launched after El Alamein. Together, the Haganah and the extremists now attacked the blockade. Soon they expanded their offensive to hit British military bases, radar stations, rail lines, and bridges, and sometimes they attacked British officials, cafés, and buses. The British countered by rounding up, imprisoning, and even executing militants, and by exiling Jewish leaders. They tightened the blockade and reinforced their army in Palestine to 100,000 men. They also deployed 4,500 men from Abdullah's Arab Legion. Still, the Jews always seemed to be a step ahead of them.

Britain's intransigence toward Zionism was clearly derived from a conviction that, weakened though it was by the war, it could retain its historic role as a power in the Middle East by tilting to the Arabs. The Arabs had more to offer in territory, bases, manpower, and, of course, oil. As the Cold War took shape, Britain also postulated that strong Arab states, like the earlier Ottoman Empire, could serve as a barrier to Russian expansion into the Mediterranean.

After its great victory at El Alamein, in fact, Britain began envisaging itself as the hub of a reorganized Middle East, with the emancipated Arab states clustered around it. It perceived no contradiction between Arab sovereignty and its own insistence on retaining military installations on Arab soil. In retrospect, it appears delusional for a fading colonial state to have imagined leading the Arabs, who had for so long seen it as the enemy, and, in time, Britain recognized how unwelcome it actually was at the Arab table. But meanwhile the Arabs, needing help in their looming conflict with Zionism, were willing to listen to what Britain was willing to offer.

In 1944 Britain placed the idea of a unified Arab bloc before a conference of seven Arab states that it convoked in Alexandria, Egypt. Islam, with its concept of the *umma,* had always encouraged unity; Arabs were by nature disposed to the idea. Though Egypt and Saudi Arabia had recently rejected Abdullah's proposal for a Greater Syria, their rejection was on the grounds that he was seeking to serve only Hashemite interests. They did not reject unity in itself.

Ironically, what the Alexandria meeting produced was drawn more from Sykes-Picot than from Islam. The Arab League, which the delegates founded there, was not synonymous with Arab unification. It was an association of sovereign states with no binding obligations to one another. If Britain saw the league as a strategic pillar, it overlooked the Arab states' penchant for mutual mistrust. Stronger than any bond of mutual obligation, this mistrust was to keep the league from becoming a significant force, even among the Arabs.

Whatever Britain offered the Arabs, this mistrust proved fatal in the war with the Jews. Egypt's solution for Palestine was a state under Hajj Amin, who had emerged as Cairo's client. Since Hajj Amin was Britain's antagonist, it was an ill-advised idea. Moreover, the Syrians and Iraqis, wary of Egypt, wanted nothing to do with Hajj Amin. All three, in addition, turned their backs on Abdullah, whom they saw as both Britain's darling and a rival claimant to Palestinian land. While the Zionists trained men, smuggled weapons, and built arms factories, the Arabs of Palestine were squeezed between putative friends, deprived of vital help by their conflicts with one another.

Zionism's insistence on sovereign statehood grew in parallel with the Jews' rising military strength. The Arabs, meanwhile, followed two contradictory courses. As sovereign states, they counted on the British to remain at their side. But as victims of colonialism, they persisted in their demand that

Britain quit the Middle East. Antagonized by Egypt's backing of Hajj Amin, London finally grasped that its strategic objectives had nothing in common with those of the Arab League. With their military contingents under relentless attack from Zionist forces, the British finally grew weary. In February 1947, they admitted failure in their three-decade effort to rule Palestine and abandoned the mandate to the United Nations.

Through most of 1947, the UN struggled to square the Palestine circle. America, the key player, hesitated to make a clear commitment to a Jewish state, popular though it was at home, out of concern for its oil supplies. But the Arabs refused to take advantage of the ambivalence of the American position. They remained self-righteous and intractably rigid, while the Jews, at the United Nations and in key world capitals, worked diligently to cultivate political support. In spurning compromise, the Arabs doomed any prospect that the world would rally to their cause.

On November 29, 1947, the UN General Assembly approved by a two-thirds vote a resolution to partition Palestine into Jewish and Arab states. The United States and the Soviet Union voted for it; Britain abstained. The only ballots in opposition came from the Arabs and an assortment of ex-colonized states. The Jews, though the resolution represented only a partial victory, accepted it enthusiastically. Rejecting it outright, the Arabs directed their anger chiefly at America, which they accused of betraying Woodrow Wilson's sacred principles. The resolution sparked a wave of hostility toward America in the Arab world, which has not since abated.

The UN resolution's passage triggered immediate resistance in Palestine. Hajj Amin ordered a general strike and took steps to unify the diverse bands that were loyal to him into the Army of Jihad, which he deployed in the center of the country. The Arab League placed its stamp on a force of volunteers and mercenaries that it called the Arab Liberation Army and moved to confront Jewish units in the north. Egypt's Muslim Brotherhood opened a front against Jewish settlements in the south. Though not nearly as well trained or led as the Jews, the combined Arab forces were at least as numerous, and they vowed a fight to the last man for the Palestinian cause.

At that point, the Americans, intimidated by the show of Arab power, surprised United Nations members by proposing to substitute a temporary international trusteeship for partition. Jews and Arabs, each confident of driving the other from the field, rejected the idea, as did most of the UN, and when Jewish units in late 1947 went on the offensive, Washington dropped the proposal. The Jews scattered the Arab forces and produced panic among Arab civilians, many of whom fled, while others were expelled from their homes. The campaign, ending in a major Arab defeat, started a tidal wave of refugees whose fate remains unresolved to this day.

On May 14, 1948, Britain completed its withdrawal from Palestine, with no provisions for a formal transfer of power. On the same day, the Zionist leadership declared the establishment of the sovereign state of Israel. The Arabs, less organized, asserted no comparable claim. In Britain's absence, the conflict in Palestine took on a new character. The Arab states formally entered the war, forcing Israel to shift its attention from the ragged Palestinian irregulars it had easily defeated to regular national armies.

Syria, Lebanon, Iraq, and Egypt each deployed several thousand men to Palestine, supported by tanks and artillery. All won some early victories. But none showed significant appetite for combat, much less a capacity for battlefield coordination, and their advances soon came to a halt. The only army that had significant success was Abdullah's legion, under the command of British officers. In savage combat that produced heavy casualties on both sides, the Arab Legion captured and held the West Bank of the Jordan and Jerusalem's Old City. His goals achieved, Abdullah withdrew from the conflict.

The fighting, twice interrupted by truces used by both sides to bring in reinforcements, lasted until January 1949, by which time Israel was in full control of most of Palestine. Abdullah by then was pursuing an objective in stark opposition to that of the other Arabs. He convened an assembly of friendly notables in the biblical city of Jericho and engineered the fusion of the West Bank, which the legion controlled, into Transjordan, which he renamed the Hashemite Kingdom of Jordan. Egypt, meanwhile, organized an All-Palestine Government in Gaza, a heavily populated strip of land between the Sinai Desert and the sea; it named Hajj Amin to govern it and persuaded Syria, Lebanon, and Iraq to recognize it. This left hostile Palestine entities—the West Bank and Gaza—confronting each other. Meanwhile, hundreds of thousands of homeless Palestinians sought refuge among Arab states whose economies were already overburdened and whose populations were themselves fragmented.

The Israelis ended the fighting by smashing Egypt's army, the Arabs' strongest, which left the remaining enemy forces too weak and demoralized to continue. An Arab-Israeli accord reached under UN sponsorship on the island of Rhodes in 1949 put a formal end to the fighting. Its terms left Israel as a cohesive, contiguous state, 20 percent larger in territory than under the United Nations' 1947 partition resolution.[3]

For Arab nationalism, the defeat of 1948 was huge. Arabs refer to it as *al-nakba*, "the catastrophe," although, as it turned out, this was not the last war to which the term was attached. It was not that the armies of the Arab states had been notably overmatched in size and equipment. It was that whatever enthusiasm Arab soldiers brought to the battlefield was nullified by the disorganization, rivalry, acrimony, incompetence, and even corruption of their leaders. After the defeat, Arabs had many questions to answer to themselves.

The chief victims of the 1948 war were the Palestinians, whose social structure simply collapsed under the pressure, creating some 750,000 refugees. The defeat left them nursing bitter grievances, not just against the Jews but against fellow Arabs. Contemplating their defeat, Arabs as a whole saw themselves as betrayed by their ruling classes and their institutions. Having shown so much strength in confronting colonialism, the Arabs had failed dismally at forging viable states, leaving them unequal to the conflict with the Jews.

The defeat shattered the Arabs' confidence, but though they had learned a lesson, they had no plan. *Al-nakba* seemed to have taught them that only radical change could drive them in a positive direction. But the tragedy did not reveal to them what the direction was.

———

Among the disillusioned Egyptians on the Palestine front was a charismatic young colonel named Gamal Abdul Nasser, who had fought hard and been wounded in battle. Like all Egyptians of his generation, Nasser was convinced that Egypt's ills were rooted in British colonialism. But he was also unsparing with Egypt's own leaders, the king, his courtiers, even the parliament, whom he considered British agents and called "the wolves who ravaged Egypt."[4] The monarchy had humiliated him as an Egyptian, by not standing up to British authority. Nasser returned home from Palestine in March 1949, just after the signing of the armistice with the Israelis. Three years later, he led the coup that brought Egypt's army to power and changed the course of Arab history.

Nasser was born in 1918, in a village named Beni Murr in the Nile Delta. His mother died when he was eight. His father, who had attended the village's first school, remarried and sent his son to be raised among relatives in Cairo and Alexandria. Nasser attended many schools as a child, without academic distinction, but after first failing the entrance exam was admitted to the Egyptian military academy on the second try. Friends described him as secretive, cautious, and puritanical, even in his youth. Anwar Sadat, born the same year as Nasser, was a fellow cadet at the academy and Nasser's successor as Egypt's leader. Sadat wrote that Nasser "was tender and loyal, full of compassion . . . but he turned into a ferocious lion the moment anyone even thought of insulting or hurting him."

In the 1930s, when Nasser and Sadat were growing up, the political climate was turbulent. Not only did the contest rage among the king, the parliament, and the British, but young people were turning to a range of radical organizations that had emerged in opposition to the state. On the right were the Muslim Brotherhood and the semifascist Young Egypt Society; on the left were the Communists and a variety of Arab socialist parties. The appeal of the Wafd's liberal, democratic nationalism, the ideal of the 1919 Revolution, had faded; the young were attracted to the radical ideologies then thriving in Europe. Tumultuous street protests were routine, assassinations common. Sadat flirted with the brotherhood, Nasser with Young Egypt.

Nasser and his generation of officers were very political. The British presence was deeply humiliating to them, especially after British tanks circled the royal palace in 1942 to coerce the king and his entourage into taking a more active role in the war. Nasser was a conscientious officer who rejected any contact with the Germans when they were at Cairo's gates. Yet Germany's defeat changed little: The British retained a garrison in the heart of Cairo, as well as 75,000 troops in the Canal Zone.

About 1944, Nasser joined the founders of the Free Officers, a secret revolutionary society in the Egyptian army, and even while fighting in Palestine he helped recruit members. Strangely, the society had little ideology, even as it laid plans for a military coup d'état. "I had sentiments which took the form of a vague hope," he once said, "then of a definite idea and finally of practical arrangements." The coup, with Nasser at its hub, took place on July 23, 1952.[5]

On the eve of the coup, huge crowds flooded Cairo's streets, demanding abrogation of the Anglo-Egyptian treaty of 1936, under which Britain claimed the right to garrison its troops on Egypt's soil. The monarchy, squeezed between colonial power and raging popular anger, finally submitted to the people and abrogated the treaty. Declaring the action void, Britain added to its forces in Egypt. America, wearing its Cold War lenses, promised to back Egypt on the treaty, on the condition it join Israel in an anti-Soviet alliance, but joining with Israel was impossible for the monarchy, or for any Arab government. When Egypt refused, Washington took the British side and the rioting intensified. Angry mobs, targeting imperialist symbols, torched much of Cairo, notably the famous opera house. Young agitators—led by Communists on the left and Muslim Brothers on the right—terrorized the streets. Dozens died. Impotent to curb the protests and without alternatives, the Egyptian regime was clearly doomed.

Most Egyptians had expected a revolution led by the street radicals. The military conspirators under Nasser were totally unknown. When the coup took place, not even the British came to the regime's defense. Most Egyptians seemed to breathe a sigh of relief at the Free Officers' revolution. Its victory was bloodless.

Once in power, the Free Officers exiled the king and dismissed the parliament, then, promisingly enough, enacted needed reforms in agriculture, commerce, and taxation. But the junta quickly turned to suppressing opposition. It shocked

Egyptians by hanging the leaders of striking workers, and it purged the higher ranks of the military and the civil service. It banned political parties and imposed limits on the press, municipalities, and professional societies. It also organized a security apparatus aimed initially at the Muslim Brotherhood, its major rival. Soon the Free Officers' security apparatus became the dominant force in Egyptian life. In 1954 the Free Officers responded to an assassination attempt on Nasser by trying a thousand dissidents for high treason; the next year the regime executed six Muslim Brothers and imprisoned three thousand. Whatever his early intentions, Nasser quickly became a despot, forging a tyranny that served as a model for discontented Arabs throughout the region.

"For years, we asked ourselves what the way was out of the monarchy and the corruption of the regime," said Naguib Mahfouz, the great novelist, in our talk in the Cairo café. "We asked, When will the people revolt? Then one morning we woke up and, frankly, I was surprised at how easily Egyptians accepted the dictatorship. I was frightened of it from the very first day. My friends and I who met for coffee at the café were angry but not brave. We knew the walls had ears, that spies were listening to us. We were persuaded by what we saw all around us to keep our opinions to ourselves. We didn't even dream of opposing Nasser."

Whatever his domestic goals, however, Nasser's revolution was directed first at Britain. Within two years of the coup, he had persuaded the colonizers to evacuate Suez, though he had to accept a proviso, in recognition of the Cold War, that British troops could return in case of an attack by the Soviet Union. Though this proviso left Nasser a Cold War hostage, getting the British out was nonetheless a victory, which promised to lay the long-standing colonial conflict to rest. It even signaled the opening of new relations with the United

States, which included the prospect of Egypt's receiving economic aid.

The Cold War, however, killed off hopes for better relations. The shadow was cast by America's proposal for another scheme to create an anti-Soviet bloc in the region. It was called the Baghdad Pact, and its intent was to raise a wall of "northern tier" states—Pakistan, Iran, Iraq, and Turkey—against Russian expansion southward. Washington avoided its earlier mistake of inviting Israel, proposing only Muslim participants to keep the issue of the Jewish state out of the debate. Moreover, it lowered its profile by letting Britain lead the negotiations. But behind the scenes, Washington made clear that it wanted the Arabs, and particularly Egypt, to take a stand in the Cold War by signing on with the West.

Nasser declined courteously at first, maintaining he had no quarrel with the Russians, who had never colonized Arab territory. He insisted, further, that Egypt had no interest in big power rivalries. His position was popular among Arabs. Egypt had, in fact, explored establishing a neutralist bloc in the Middle East, composed of the Arab League states and Turkey, free of the Cold War. In discussions on the Baghdad Pact, Nasser asked Washington to understand that Egypt could not leap overnight from being Britain's colony to being its military ally. It needed time, he said, to convalesce "in complete independence." When America dismissed his logic, Nasser turned his back on the scheme in order to make himself the champion of a "no-pacts" strategy among the Arab states.

"Nonalignment" was the description given to Nasser's position at Bandung, Indonesia, in 1955, when he joined India's Jawaharlal Nehru and China's Chou En-lai to establish a neutralist bloc. America's response was to treat the new bloc as an enemy. John Foster Dulles, the U.S. secretary of state, called nonalignment "an immoral and short-sighted conception." United States policy, in demanding an unequivocal anti-Communism, wound up only poisoning relations between the nonaligned states and the West.

But it was rising strife with Israel, even more than neutralism, that drew Nasser into the Soviet camp. Recurring raids on Israeli settlements by Palestinian *fedayeen* (self-sacrificers) from bases in Egyptian-ruled Gaza had created a pattern of bloody conflict. Unwilling—or perhaps unable—to curb the *fedayeen,* Nasser petitioned London and Washington for arms to counter Israel's retaliation. Both declined to help him, leading him to turn to Moscow. The arrival in Egypt in 1956 of Soviet planes, tanks, and ships dramatically reversed the course of reconciliation with the West on which Nasser two years earlier had embarked.

The breach over Soviet arms transformed negotiations on American help to Egypt in financing the Aswan Dam. Since taking power, the Free Officers had dreamed of building a high dam on the Upper Nile to augment Egypt's electrical generating capacity and its arable farmland. When Moscow and Washington dangled competing offers to finance it, Nasser vacillated. In the midst of the bargaining, Britain carried out its pledge to withdraw from Suez, and Egypt's relations with the West seemed to improve. Nasser decided to go with Washington's bid, but by the time he announced his acceptance, the arms deal had been concluded. America then informed Nasser that the offer had been withdrawn.

Punishing Nasser was America's signal to the world that it would not abide nonalignment, much less a military tie to the Soviet Union. Furious, Nasser retaliated by nationalizing the Suez Canal Company. Since Britain and France were the company's chief stockholders, as well as the canal's principal users, they were more directly affected than Washington by the change in its status. Independently of America, the two began laying plans to deal with Nasser, then raised the ante by inviting Israel to join them.

On October 29, 1956, Israeli air and land forces attacked Egypt. Within a few days, Israel had captured the Gaza Strip and much of the Sinai Desert, along with thousands of Egyptian prisoners and a storehouse of Russian military equipment. Behind a façade of fairness, Britain and France issued an ultimatum demanding that both sides withdraw their forces. Israel's rejection was preplanned; Egypt's rejection was based on the British-French insistence that it evacuate its own territory, which was clearly inadmissible. Days later an Anglo-French paratroop force dropped on Suez and advanced southward along the banks of the canal.

The United States followed with a surprising step, breaking the rules of the Cold War to line up with the Soviet Union at the United Nations in demanding an immediate cease-fire. Britain and France vetoed the U.S. resolution. Faithful to Arab League customs, no Arab state volunteered to come to Egypt's defense, but Russia threatened its own military intervention. Washington warned that if it happened, war would follow.

With events spinning out of control, Washington announced a decision to impose a withdrawal on its allies. Under tremendous pressure, Britain and France agreed to evacuate their units in favor of a United Nations Emergency Force. With Nasser's approval, the force took positions on Egypt's side of the border. Israel held out longer than the British and French, demanding that Egypt, in return for its evacuation, lift the blockade of its southern port of Elath. Washington rejected the condition, though in its place it offered vague assurance of a right of passage through the narrow Strait of Tiran on the way to Elath. In March 1967, Israel, too, withdrew from Egyptian territory. At the time, the terms of its withdrawal seemed ordinary enough; a decade later the American assurance of Elath's accessibility would be crucial to igniting an even bigger war.

The Suez campaign was the last gasp of British and French colonialism in the Middle East, and it ended with America indisputably the region's most influential power. But it also intensified the West's contest with the Soviet Union for the Arabs' Cold War allegiance. The Arabs gave the United States little credit for its harsh treatment of its allies, the old imperial states. Most Arabs, in fact, criticized America for having started the trouble in the first place by provoking Nasser over the Aswan Dam. In the end, the Suez affair not only undermined whatever credibility the West retained among the Arabs but did irreversible damage to America in the Cold War competition.

The Suez attack also weakened the West's friends among Arab leaders. Among them were Jordan's recently crowned King Hussein, grandson of King Abdullah, and the Iraqis loyal to Iraq's Hashemite dynasty. Suez exposed them to the charge, deftly exploited by Nasser, of being not just pro-colonial but pro-Israel. After the attack, Nasser gravitated deeper into the Soviet camp, while America stumbled over the diplomatic debris that the Suez campaign had left.

Washington seemingly failed to grasp the damage done by the Suez attack. In continuing to demand that the Arabs choose the West over Russia, it took a righteous gamble, and, measured by the response of the Arab masses, it lost. Woodrow Wilson had long ago lost his place as a hero among Arabs. Suez confirmed America, in Arab eyes, as the heir to the Western imperial tradition. Even today, with the Cold War long over, America has not reversed that perception.

It was a paradox of the Suez campaign that Nasser, despite his dismal showing as a warrior, emerged an idol of the Arab masses. Having cheered him for Britain's departure in 1954, they saw Suez two years later as meaning even more. The retreat from Suez of the great European powers was taken, however illusorily, as the end of the long, bitter sequence of Western victories over the Arabs. Israel's forced withdrawal was an added gift. The masses did not register that Washington had coerced its own allies in their behalf. Exultant crowds filled the streets of Arab cities, denouncing America while celebrating Nasser's triumph.

Nasser's ambition, fed by the popular enthusiasm, soared after Suez. He cast caution aside. Suddenly, he perceived himself as not just Egypt's leader but the engine of Arab regeneration. In his intoxication, he urged Arabs to forgo their narrow loyalties in favor of Pan-Arabism, *al-qawmiyya,* "the Arab nation from the Atlantic Ocean to the Arabian Gulf."[6] By unifying in a single, powerful state, he proclaimed, the Arabs under his leadership would restore their ancient grandeur.

Nasser gave the Pan-Arab idea, largely dormant since Sharif Hussein's era, a new life; it would dominate Arab politics in the years after Suez. By the skillful use of modern communications, Nasser spread its message throughout the region. His charisma exercised magic over the masses longing for guidance. In Arab ruling circles it struck fear. In the end, however, the fiery nationalism that Nasser proclaimed turned out to be empty words. He deluded a civilization whose weaknesses—poverty, illiteracy, religiosity, chronic corruption, and misrule—he failed to address. But for a time he appeared impregnable. For the next decade and a half, his leadership would have a profound impact everywhere in the Arab world.

V

UNITY-DISUNITY

1957-1967

Stepping into the void left by the humiliation of Britain and France at Suez, the United States involved itself more energetically than before in the Middle East. The intensity of the Cold War was rising. In the year of Suez, the Soviet Union showed in Hungary its willingness to use armed force to preserve its hegemony within the Communist bloc. Having placed into space *Sputnik I*, the first artificial satellite, it was feeling expansive. Washington could hardly be indifferent to the progress the USSR was making in winning support in the Arab world.

President Dwight Eisenhower, in an address to Congress in March 1957, overlooked the vestiges of Western imperialism, as well as inherent weakness among the Arabs, to blame "International Communism" for the region's drift away from the West. "Russia's interest in the Middle East is solely that of power politics," he said. Moscow's design was to dominate the region, he warned, as part of its "announced purpose of Communizing the world." In what became a doctrine that took his name, Eisenhower asserted America's right to use armed force against Russia or "any nation controlled by International Communism" to preserve its interests in the region.[1]

Syria was particularly outspoken in denouncing the Eisenhower Doctrine, arguing that its quarrel was not with Communism but with Zionism and imperialism. Recently, fifty-six of its soldiers had been killed in a border skirmish with Israel. Washington did not respond but Moscow offered Syria the consolation of money and arms. Obsessed with the Cold War, the United States attached little importance to Syria's conflict with Israel or with the West.

In the spring of 1957, Damascus brought a complaint to the United Nations that Turkey, America's ally, was threatening an invasion. A few weeks later, Syria expelled three American diplomats on charges—for which it produced some evidence—of seeking to overthrow the government. Still, Washington refused to consider the possibility that Syria's concerns were legitimately nationalist, and that it was tilting toward Communism only by default.

It is worth noting that since the Palestine debacle of 1948, Syria's system of government had been in disarray. French colonialism had created a democratic structure, which Syria's elected leaders had used astutely in the 1930s in the struggle for freedom from France. But Syrians, accustomed to thinking of Palestinians as their southern countrymen, felt a strong bond with Palestine, and the government's bungling performance in the 1948 war discredited not only their democratically elected leaders but democracy itself. After 1948, Syrians grew dubious about whether their democracy would work in normal times.

Syrians from all sectors, out of a hope for a more decisive government, seemed to rejoice when the army conducted a coup d'état against their democracy in 1949. Military rule seemed to provide a comfortable cultural fit but, in fact, the army proved to be no better than the parliamentarians at governing. The first military regime lasted only months before giving way to a second, which restored a parliamentary structure beneath military cover. Then the army struck again in 1951 to establish a full-fledged dictatorship. In 1954 military units reinstated the democratic system, but Syrians were by now tired of the revolving door and wanted real stability.

In the aftermath of the Suez crisis, the army was still dominant, but other forces had emerged to compete for power. The Communist Party, benefiting from Russia's transfer of money and arms, had widened its popular base but, whatever

Washington's misgivings about Syrians, many saw danger in becoming beholden to Moscow. Support for the Muslim Brotherhood had grown with its denunciations of the Suez campaign and Western infidels, but many Syrians were also suspicious of state religion. The Ba'ath Party, a new faction, was attracting a rising following with a Pan-Arabist ideology that embraced both Muslims and Christians, but it had yet to sink roots in the society. Though each group was suspicious of the others, all—even the old republicans—agreed that the chief threat to the Arabs and to Syria came from Cold War America. By 1957, Nasser's anti-Americanism and his call for Arab unity offered an ideology that much of Syria thought addressed the country's problems.

The Syrian army took the initiative in wooing Nasser, sending repeated delegations to Cairo. Nasser received them warmly. To show his goodwill, he even sent troops to Syria to stand against the possible Turkish invasion. Nasser knew that if he was to succeed in leading a unification movement, he needed Syria, hub of the Arab heartland. But his terms were all or nothing. Nasser would have no truck with a system in which Syrian organizations, even the army, retained power. His plan was to shape an Arab union on the model of Egypt's despotism. He knew that once Syria's army accepted his conditions, neither the hollow parliamentary regime nor the opposition parties could stand against him. His strategy succeeded. On February 1, 1958, Egypt and Syria proclaimed their amalgamation into the United Arab Republic.[2]

Under the unification agreement, the new state—commonly known as the UAR—brought Egypt and Syria together as equals. In reality, however, the UAR subsumed Syria's political identity into that of Egypt. All power derived from Nasser, the president. Syria complied with Nasser's demand that it dissolve its legislature and political parties, institutions that he insisted were divisive. In a plebiscite, the UAR received the endorsement of nearly 100 percent of the voters in both Syria and Egypt.

But the appearance of unity was deceiving, and the United Arab Republic lasted only three years. In that time, Syrians learned to distinguish between Pan-Arabism, the drive for Arab unity, and the peculiar version that came to be called Nasserism, the ideology of a rigidly militarist and authoritarian state, in which only one man's word was law.

Nasser treated Syria as his private province. He named Egyptians faithful to him to the top offices. He selected only a handful of Syrians among the six hundred handpicked deputies to the national assembly. He dispatched Egyptian loyalists to run the civil service, and even the schools. He confiscated land and socialized commerce, a huge blow to Syria's merchant class. He even crippled the Ba'ath Party, though its own Pan-Arabist ideology and its political support had been crucial to his success. In insisting on total power, Nasser himself was the chief factor in the UAR's collapse.

The explanation for the failure of Arab unity, however, probably goes deeper than that. Though Islam promotes the cohesion of the *umma,* the Muslim community, Arabs have always been riven by political rivalries. Cairo, Baghdad, and Damascus have historically represented competing poles of power. Under the Ottomans, governing in Istanbul, Baghdad and Damascus were humiliated in being reduced to provincial cities, while Cairo, having won its autonomy, ruled over a strong, virtually independent state. Only after World War I, thanks to the frontiers drawn by Sykes and Picot to serve the objectives of Western colonialism, did Syria and Iraq acquire a sense of their own nationhood. When they did, their suspicion of Egypt remained.

Not surprisingly, Syria and Iraq produced leaders with vested interests not in Arab unity but in statehood. The roles of these leaders in society, and often their income, depended on the sovereign entities they led. In the UAR, Nasser ignored both the Syrians' discomfort at accepting submission to Cairo and the price the leadership paid in being divested of power. It was a major lapse on his part. Given the inherent flaws in its structure, the UAR could not survive.

On September 28, 1961, army officers overthrew the Egyptian rule and declared Syria's independence from Cairo. They arrested Egypt's principal military and civilian chiefs in Damascus and sent them home. Egypt's forces in Syria put up some resistance, and about fifty died in the fighting, but their numbers were too few to resist the separation. Daunted by the prospect of conducting a distant war, Nasser decided within a few days to accept the reversal.

Syria's victorious military junta renamed the country the Syrian Arab Republic and turned power over to a civilian cabinet. Syria rejoined the Arab League. The country's masses, having for years absorbed Nasserist propaganda, did not openly rejoice but made no protests. The other Arab regimes, threatened by Nasser, were secretly relieved by his defeat and the restoration of Syria's statehood.

Still, the UAR's demise did not resolve the issue of Syria's future. The provisional cabinet authorized a free election, in which a conservative parliament was chosen, and which rolled back some of the Nasser era's radical measures. But a few months later the regime was overthrown in another military coup, which reinstated old Nasserist laws. The revolving door was moving again. The signs, moreover, indicated that, while Syrians had rejected Nasser's despotism, they had not tired of the Pan-Arabism he stood for. On the Syrian terrain, Pan-Arabism was now represented by the Ba'ath Party.

Hafez al-Assad, soon to be the dominant power in Syrian politics, was born into a family of Alawite peasants and joined the Ba'ath Party when he was sixteen. It was no coincidence that, in a society that is preponderantly Sunni Muslim, most

Ba'athis were from minority groups—Alawite, Christian, Kurd, Druze, and Ismaili. Ba'athism's founders were mostly Christian, and their vision was popular reconciliation, emphasizing not Islam but a shared Arabism. The party was especially strong in the armed forces, which ambitious minority youths used as a vehicle of social advancement. Assad entered the air force's flying school in 1951, and by the time he graduated, four years later, was already at a professional and social level attained by few Alawites. During advanced flight training in Cairo, he was exposed to the magnetism of Nasser, but he was no disciple. On returning to Syria, he joined with four fellow officers—two Alawites, two Ismailis—to plot a Ba'athi overthrow of the weak, post-UAR regime.

Assad's group conducted a successful coup in March 1963, and, after months of fighting for power, he emerged the winner. Though only in his thirties and a captain, he exercised power by the force of his personality and through his control of the air force. In a bloody putsch in 1966, he and his friends eliminated the party's liberal elements and ended meaningful elections. Under his direction, Ba'athism was transformed from a civilian and parliamentary movement to a military, authoritarian, and radical force. By 1970 Assad had taken personal command of both the party and the regime, and presided in making the state bureaucratic, stodgy, and brutal. Still, in the 1960s, when the revolution was young, the breath that Ba'athism emitted seemed to offer strength with the oxygen of freedom, for which Syrians were grateful.

Almost simultaneous with the Ba'ath triumph in Syria, the Iraqi Ba'ath Party—despite their obvious rivalry, the two insisted they were a single body with separate regional commands—seized power in a coup in Baghdad. The victory seemed a triumph of ideals that were destined to unify them into a single Arab state. Instead, the ancient competition between Damascus and Baghdad, as well as conflict between personalities, would keep Syria and Iraq in permanent confrontation, while the ideal of Arab unity served as a cover for creeping tyranny. Ba'athi government brought stability but no unity to the *mashreq*. In Syria, as in Iraq, the Ba'athis would become better known for the iron fist that would dominate the population, keeping both regimes in power.

———

Lebanon's political system emerged from the Palestine war of 1948 in surprisingly sound condition. France had founded Lebanon in the 1920s by separating the Ottomans' Christian enclave, with which it had relations dating back to the Middle Ages, from the Ottoman province of Syria. France then added Syrian Muslims to the new country on the theory that numbers would add to its strength. The regime that France established was dominated by Christians, which outraged the Muslims. But, more damaging, the arrangement produced not a strong Lebanon but a country split into hostile fragments. The Christians were oriented westward to Europe, the Muslims eastward to the Arab heartland, and each was itself divided into antagonistic factions. During World War II, when France's influence all but vanished, Lebanon's prospects for successful self-government seemed extremely slim.

Then, in 1943, the Lebanese made an effort to deal with the matter themselves. They adopted a plan they called the National Pact. Though elections were at its base, it was not a blueprint for democracy. Indeed, had Lebanon opted for a strict majoritarian system, every election would have been a sectarian contest, with life-or-death risks. Instead, the Lebanese devised a complex structure that conceded Christian dominance while allocating shares of power among the sectarian subgroups. The system was called "confessionalism," and though none of the factions was fully satisfied, all of them were accorded a stake in it. By emerging intact from the 1948 war, Lebanon seemed to show that the system worked.

Lebanese society, however, remained volatile. Decisions were reached by a handful of elite families, both Christian and Muslim, who often showed more concern for their own interests than for the country's. Meanwhile, the gap widened between rich and poor. In 1952 Egypt's revolution aroused a few Lebanese reformers to stage an insurrection, which ended with some new faces in office but little social or political change. Christians remained constitutionally preponderant and disproportionately wealthy, while the Muslim masses grew poorer and more resentful. The Cold War, and the attendant rise of Nasserism among the Muslims, added to the difficulties of preserving the society's equilibrium.

In 1955, the Christians showed their muscle by announcing Lebanon's acceptance, in return for economic aid, of America's invitation to join the Baghdad Pact. The Arab League objected angrily; Syria, having never reconciled to Lebanon's detachment thirty years earlier, threatened to retaliate. But Lebanon's Christian-dominated government remained resolutely pro-American, and in 1956 it was the only Arab state that did not sever relations with the European invaders of Suez. Lebanon also bowed to the Eisenhower Doctrine, which promised American military support to preserve the country's independence. Clearly, Lebanon's Christians were isolating it from the Arab world.

Predictably, Lebanon's Muslim masses grew increasingly rebellious, and intoxicated by Nasser's oratory. Pan-Arabism became the rage among Lebanese Muslims, and portraits of Nasser appeared on the walls of Muslim quarters throughout the country. In 1958, when Egypt and Syria formed the UAR, defiant Muslims took to the streets to demand that Lebanon join. On both the Christian and Muslim sides of the political divide, radicals became more strident and the spirit of conciliation retreated.

The National Pact of 1943 appeared to be in shambles

when Christian-Muslim violence broke out in May 1958, three months after the Egyptian-Syrian union. Though the fighting surpassed that of the modest 1952 uprising, Lebanon's army, as fragmented as the country itself, abdicated any role in restoring calm. The UAR's deliveries of arms and munitions to Lebanon's Nasserists aggravated the situation. Whether Nasser planned to absorb Lebanon into the UAR, as many charged, has never been confirmed. But Washington, with its Cold War priorities, feared that Lebanon would fall to Nasserism, which it regarded as equivalent to Communism, and it did not intend to take a chance.

Lebanon's civil war in mid-1958, simultaneous with a rebellion in Jordan and the overthrow of the monarchy in Iraq, persuaded Washington that Nasserism threatened to blow up the entire region. Invoking the Eisenhower Doctrine, the United States landed 3,600 Marines in Beirut on July 15, 1958. Its declared aim was to preserve Lebanon's sovereignty, but its presence ensured the survival of the Christian-dominated, pro-Western regime. Syria decried the landing, and the Nasserist rebels threatened to attack. But, in fact, the Americans not only met no resistance but were warmly received on the beaches. It was a measure of Lebanon's cultural divide that the navy reported bikini-clad young women—surely Christian, since Muslim girls would not have dressed that way—cheering as the leathernecks waded ashore.[3]

Before the U.S. forces withdrew from Lebanon in October, American diplomats helped arrange a reconciliation between the rebels and the regime. The agreement essentially restored the terms of the 1943 National Pact. Washington regarded the state's survival as the vindication for the invasion, but Lebanon's basic problems, political and social, had not been touched. Moreover, America's wider goal was unmet. Lebanon was calm, but the uprising in Iraq had brought to power a radical military government, and the outbreak in Jordan was uncontained. Nasserism was still on the move, which Washington understood to mean that the West had failed to stop the Arab world's gravitation toward Moscow.

———

Of the Arab leaders who participated in the Palestine war, Jordan's King Abdullah was alone in having achieved his aims. After the fighting, his armed forces held East Jerusalem and the West Bank, which, with their Palestinian inhabitants, he proceeded to annex. The annexation proved a mixed blessing. On the one hand, it made Jordan a more significant power in Arab affairs. On the other, in transforming Jordan into a heterogeneous kingdom of Jordanians and Palestinians, it replaced tranquillity with turbulence, which would soon cost Abdullah his life and his heirs unremitting woe.

The 1948 war in Palestine had tripled Jordan's population, largely with destitute refugees, sullen over their fate. They were suspicious of the Hashemites for their ongoing ties with the British and for the sympathy they had displayed over the decades to the Jews. They brought an angry Palestinian nationalism to Jordan, and many were still loyal to Hajj Amin, though the war had been a disaster for his followers. On July 20, 1951, an angry acolyte of Hajj Amin assassinated Abdullah in Jerusalem, where he had gone to pay homage at the grave of Sharif Hussein, his father.

Abdullah was succeeded, after a brief interval, by his teenage grandson Hussein, who had been with him in Jerusalem on the day of the assassination. Product of a British education, Hussein was instinctively pro-Western in political outlook. He assumed the throne in 1953, at age eighteen, soon after Nasser came to power. Nasser wasted no time in pressuring him to emulate Egypt by abrogating Jordan's treaty relations with Britain. It would have been understandable, considering the angry Palestinians in his kingdom, had the young monarch taken Nasser's advice. His refusal, in a time of rising Nasserism and intensifying Cold War, meant that, like Lebanon, Jordan was likely to survive only by juggling its allegiance tirelessly between the Arab world and the West.

Hussein's initial impulse was to reaffirm Jordan's parliamentary democracy, but Nasserism had made the parliament little more than an arena for screeds against the throne. So he dissolved the parliament, which added to his reliance on Abdullah's old political base, Britain and the Bedouin tribes. The poverty of the refugees had made Jordan more needy than ever of Britain's subsidy, but accepting the subsidy made the king more vulnerable to Nasserist assaults. Meanwhile, attacks by Palestinian terrorists on Israel, endorsed by Nasser, elicited reprisals in Jordan, adding to the fragility of the throne.

Jordan reached the edge of the abyss when Washington provoked the crisis with the Arabs over the Baghdad Pact. The king first straddled the issue, satisfying no one. When riots broke out in Jordanian cities, Britain threw him a life preserver by raising his subsidy, but Egypt countered by offering him Arab funds. The king zigged toward the Arabs, declaring his rejection of the Baghdad Pact and dismissing the revered British general Sir John Glubb as commander of the Arab Legion. But then he zagged, spurning Nasser's money and reaffirming his relationship with his British patron. Taking personal command of the heavily Bedouin army, Hussein succeeded in suppressing the riots and restoring order.

But his situation deteriorated again in 1956, in the wake of the attack on Suez. Though Hussein broke ties with France, he kept the door to Britain open. By breaking the old ties, Britain had discreetly informed him, there would be no more subsidy. The king's half measure provoked the local Nasserists, who pleaded with Egypt to reaffirm its monetary offer. The crisis ended when Nasser reneged.

In 1957 Nasserist sympathizers in Jordan's army twice attempted coups against the king. In the more serious of them,

Hussein rushed to an army base personally to rally his loyal Bedouins. His courage defeated the coups but did not end the crises.

In 1958, when Nasser joined with Syria in the UAR, King Hussein and his cousin King Faisal II of Iraq, both descendants of Sharif Hussein, perceived a new danger and established a defensive alliance called the Arab Federation, unfurling as its emblem the flag of the Arab Revolt. Both recognized that Nasserists were not their only enemy. The two thrones had been targeted by other factions, including Communists and Muslim Brothers. But before the two kings could organize the federation for action, the entire Middle East was in flames. The civil war had broken out in Lebanon, and the United States had landed the Marines in Beirut. Britain sent a brigade of paratroops from Cyprus to Jordan to reinforce King Hussein. Though Western power preserved the status quo in Jordan and Lebanon, that was not the case in Iraq. When the Iraqi army revolted in July, the Western powers were too far from Baghdad to respond. The uprising did away with the monarchy, setting off repercussions that are still being felt.

———

Iraq's parliamentary monarchy had not seemed in jeopardy through most of the 1950s. The uneasy mix of Sunnis, Shi'ites, and Kurds that the Treaty of Sèvres had squeezed into a state, along with a few Christians, Turkmen, and Jews, had proven surprisingly resilient. Iraq's Hashemite throne, its links with Britain still intact, remained the unifying factor in the state. Though regimes had fallen in Egypt and Syria, most Iraqis presumed their system, having survived a series of pitfalls, would outlast Nasserism, too.

Iraq, in fact, seemed to have overcome sectarianism. Though the ruling elite remained preponderantly Sunni, the Shi'ite majority seemed content to live with the crumbs of power. The Kurds, exhausted by their earlier rebellions, had adopted a live-and-let-live position. Political disputes, though contentious, were generally resolved within parliamentary bounds. The Communists created an exception. As in Syria, the party had been legitimized by Moscow's anti-imperialism, complemented by Nasser's pro-Soviet tilt. The party was too secular for the masses, drawing most of its support from society's outcasts. But the government tolerated the Communists until their demonstrations leaped out of control, then dealt with them savagely.

Since Prince Faisal became king after World War I, Iraq had been governed by basically the same conservative bloc, whose most prominent member was Nuri Said. Born in 1888, son of an Ottoman civil servant, Nuri was educated at the military academy in Istanbul. He was one of the first Ottoman officers during the Arab Revolt to throw in his lot with Faisal. He served the Hashemite throne long and faithfully, always pushing it in a pro-Western direction. Even when the infant Faisal II became king in 1939 and Prince Abd al-Ilah, his uncle, exercised the powers of the throne as regent, Nuri remained the pillar of the regime. Over the years, the army served as Nuri's personal power base. But relations began to grow tense as the generation of ex-Ottoman officers who had founded the army gave way to a new generation of Arab nationalists, resolutely anti-Western.

As long as he had the backing of the throne and the army, Nuri seemed invulnerable. His competence, ruthlessness, courage, and charm won him the respect even of his political opponents. In the 1930s, steering the monarchy through its delicate negotiations for independence, he was the Arabs' most successful leader, persuading Britain to withdraw its military bases. When Faisal II came of age in 1953 and terminated Abd al-Ilah's regency, Nuri stayed on to serve him. Most Iraqis believed that, as long as Nuri was there, the monarchy was safe.

But Nuri's fidelity to the West betrayed him in the negotiations over the Baghdad Pact, in which he was more than a bystander. Nuri may even have initiated the idea of a "northern tier" of Islamic states to contain the Russians, whom he considered dangerous not just to the West but to Iraq. Dismayed Arabs rushed to persuade him that the Baghdad Pact was an insult in offering the British an excuse to return to the Arab world as occupiers. Nuri, however, took full responsibility, shepherding the agreement through Iraq's parliament and presiding personally over the dedication of its headquarters in Baghdad.

In 1956 the Suez attack shattered Nuri's effort to tighten Iraq's Western links further. Not even he could defend the Anglo-French invasion of Egypt. On the contrary, Nuri declared Iraqi solidarity with Egypt, severed ties with France, and barred Britain from meetings of the Baghdad Pact countries. But it was too late to shift his identity as a collaborator with the West.

Suez was a gift to Iraq's rising Nasserist movement. Egyptian radio intensified its antigovernment propaganda, and, in response to mass demonstrations, Nuri brutally applied martial law. When Syria joined Egypt in the UAR in February 1958, he responded by tying Iraq to Jordan in the Arab Federation, then sidestepped the Hashemites' historic quarrel with the Sauds to solicit their protection. But he could not dispel the Iraqi regime's pro-Western taint.

On July 14, 1958, Iraqi army commanders conducted a coup d'état. Ordered into defensive positions against an attack from Syria, they instead surrounded the royal palace in Baghdad. King Faisal II, Abd al-Ilah, and much of the Hashemite family, who were seized trying to flee, were shot on the spot. Nuri, disguised in a black *abaya*, escaped from his home but was captured by a mob and murdered. The next day surging crowds, killing and looting uncontrollably, disinterred his body and dragged it through the streets.

Though only a few officers were involved in the action, the behavior of the mobs left little doubt that the coup corresponded with popular feelings. It is probable Iraqis were not so much anti-Hashemite as anti-West, but the two had in time become indistinguishable. Arab nationalism's triumph in Baghdad was decisive. Even had the West been so disposed, the coup came too abruptly to permit Western military intervention. The revolutionaries brought Rashid Ali, leader of the anti-British uprising in 1941, home from exile as the symbol of the coup's historic legitimacy.

The leader of the coup was Brigadier Abdul Karim Kassim, who named himself head of both the ruling junta and the army. Though predominantly Sunni like its predecessor, the regime proclaimed Pan-Arabism as its theme. Within a few days, it dispatched a delegation to Cairo, where Nasser publicly pledged his fraternal support. Iraq withdrew formally from the Baghdad Pact and established relations with the Soviet Union. Nuri's limitations on local Communists were relaxed, Western companies were expelled from the country, and Nasser-style economic reforms were decreed.

Law and order, however, remained elusive, and for weeks aggressive mobs chased down monarchists, killing many and turning others over to kangaroo courts. Some Iraqis, in retrospect, say the breakdown of order during the revolution initiated a taste for violence that has lasted until this day.

Kassim, meanwhile, made no move to accommodate the Pan-Arabists who vowed to unite Iraq with Egypt and Syria in a grander UAR. Iraqi public opinion, as far as it was measurable, did not demand the union. With the monarchy gone, the Pan-Arabism that Iraq's masses had once cheered in the streets seemed theoretical. In practice, most revolutionaries showed a greater disposition to embrace a strong but narrow Iraqi nationalism. Kassim, for his part, was clearly loath to share power with Egyptians, much less to follow the Syrian precedent of accepting subordination to Nasser's one-man rule.

Some of Kassim's revolutionary collaborators, however, objected to his reticence, but none more than Iraq's Ba'athis, the most extreme of the Pan-Arabist factions. At the opposite pole stood the Communists. Being not Pan-Arabist at all, they feared the influence of Nasser, a relentless persecutor of the Communists in Egypt. Pulled in opposite directions by Ba'athis and Communists, Kassim chose the latter as the base of his support. It was to prove a fatal mistake.

The Communists, though not the largest, were then Iraq's best-organized political force. They stood by Kassim in March 1959 in suppressing an uprising of troops demanding a reassertion of Pan-Arab purity. Seeking a wider reach, they then allied with Kurdish dissidents, to whom the revolution offered a chance to achieve their own national goals. In July, a year after the revolution, Communists and Kurds undertook a military offensive to seize the levers of state power. The army defeated it, but the alliance exposed Kassim's ideological weakness. No regime dependent on Communists and Kurds could endure in Iraq. In October 1959, a Ba'athi hit squad led by a young tough named Saddam Hussein shot and wounded Kassim on a Baghdad street. Though he survived, he by now had too little popular support to save his government.

Kassim took a last gamble to regain the initiative in mid-1961, after Britain granted independence to Kuwait, its colony at Iraq's southern tip. Ordering troops to the border, Kassim declared that Kuwait, having been within Basra province under the Ottomans, was legally part of Iraq. Facing invasion, Kuwait summoned British forces to return; a few weeks later, Britain withdrew them in favor of Arab League units. Though he derided the Arab League as a Western puppet, Kassim had gone too far. Overthrown in February 1963 by a Ba'athi coup, he and his entourage were summarily executed.[4]

Ba'athis now ruled both Iraq and Syria. The three most powerful Arab states—Nasser's Egypt, Syria, and Iraq—were committed to a Pan-Arab ideology. So, apparently, were the Arab masses. Yet the unification that had once seemed inevitable never occurred. Like Kassim five years earlier, Iraqi and Syrian Ba'athis rejected subordination to Nasser, and Nasser could not conceive of unification in any other terms. Pan-Arabism was trumped by the more conventional nationalism that emerged from the maps drawn by Western imperialists after World War I. Each of the Arab countries held firm to its own national identity.

Pan-Arabism's failure demonstrated that Arabs could pledge their bond to the Arab community, to the *umma*, while at the same time embracing the nationalism of the state in which they lived, whose passport they carried, where their families were rooted. In Arabic terms, rather than having to choose between *al-wataniyya* and *al-qawmiyya*, Arabs regarded the two as complementary. Arabs were at ease in the 1960s giving their loyalty to Pan-Arabism as an ideology, without surrendering their identity as Iraqis, Syrians, or Egyptians. Most seem to feel that way today.

The Pan-Arabists did not readily concede defeat for their ideology. In Syria, the Ba'ath Party has continued to run the country as a conventional nation-state while mouthing Pan-Arab slogans. In Iraq, the Ba'athis were briefly dislodged in a countercoup in 1964 but returned and remained in power until the U.S. invasion of 2003. Through the long, cruel reign of Saddam Hussein, Iraqis talked of Arab unity but did nothing to make it happen. The two Ba'athi states, Syria and Iraq, long thrived giving only lip service to Pan-Arabism. Among the Pan-Arabists, only Nasser was prematurely undone, drawn by his own hubris into monumental miscalculations.

———

Whatever his vision of national unity, Nasser turned out to be a hugely divisive force among the Arabs. He threw in the lot of the Arabs with the loser in the Cold War while deliberately stretching the breach between Arabs and the West. His Pan-Arab conception, linked to his own version of socialism, became the instrument of a personal despotism that forced a wedge between Arabs. Nasser's oratory intoxicated the crowds, but his achievement fell disastrously short. The Arabs still have not recovered from his misjudgments.

Unsuccessful in the 1950s and early 1960s in pulling Syria and Iraq into his net, Nasser found a new prospect in Yemen, a mountainous, largely Bedouin state at the base of Arabia. In a coup in September 1962, officers of the Yemeni army, portraying themselves as Nasserists, overthrew the country's ruling imam and declared a republic. Yemen's tribes, however, rallied to their traditional leader and, within a month, the uprising was in trouble. Entreated for help, Nasser overlooked the lesson of Jordan, where Bedouin tribes had shown a clear preference for their traditional chiefs. He sent Egyptian forces to support Yemen's revolutionaries.

Nasser also failed to take account of the presence of Britain and the Saudis nearby. The British operated a naval base in Aden, a longtime colony abutting Yemen, and Aden had a rising Nasserist movement of its own. Saudi Arabia, a conservative monarchy at odds with all that Nasser represented, feared his aim was to extend his secular authoritarianism to the entire Arabian peninsula. Britain and the Saudis met the Nasser challenge by supplying Yemen's tribesmen with money and arms.

Inevitably, the Cold War also made an impact. Prodded by Moscow, Nasser had his Yemeni ally sign a treaty of friendship with the Soviet bloc, though the treaty provided the rebels with little military support. In response, the American government of John F. Kennedy, while loath to dispatch forces of its own to the conflict, pressed the United Nations to take on the task. In Nasser's view, the move constituted Western intimidation, making him even more determined to prevail.

By the mid-1960s, some eighty thousand Egyptian troops, backed by air units, had been deployed to Yemen and, step by step, they had assumed the full burden of the fighting. But badly led and unfamiliar with the climate and the terrain, they suffered huge losses, while Egyptian society was burdened with crushing costs.

Perceiving Egypt's vulnerability, the United States and Britain funneled more weapons to the Yemeni loyalists. The revolutionaries, having lost confidence in Nasser's capacity to win the war, now turned on one another. Despite the deterioration, however, Nasser kept on, until he made a still greater miscalculation in 1967 in provoking a war with Israel.[5]

Nasser's defeats in Yemen lured him into a trap. Syria and Jordan had turned the tables on his years of taunts by mocking him for his fumbling. They also mocked him, more painfully, for his empty boasts that he would soon liberate Palestine.

In the spring of 1967, skirmishes with Israel on the borders of Syria and Jordan had roused tensions throughout the Middle East. Neither country wanted war, and both understood that Nasser, with his army bogged down in Yemen, was in no position to take Israel on. Still, they sneered at him for hiding behind the United Nations Emergency Force, which had been stationed in Egypt in the aftermath of the 1956 Suez attack. Nasser "is the only Arab leader," declared Amman radio, "who lives in peace and tranquillity with Israel. . . . This is a disgrace." Finally, Nasser took the bait.

On May 28, 1967, he demanded that the United Nations remove its force from Egypt's territory. Historians still debate whether the UN, aware that its departure was likely to ignite a war, had the power to refuse, or at least to delay, compliance.

They also debate whether Nasser wanted the UN to refuse. But, whatever the answers, the UN followed the letter of its agreement with Egypt and consented to depart.

For the first time since Suez, Nasser then moved troops into the Sinai, positioning them to reestablish the blockade of Israel's port of Elath. The United States, deeply embroiled in Vietnam, chose to disregard the pledge it had made after Suez to safeguard Elath's approaches. Snagged by their own rhetoric, Syria and Jordan submitted to Nasser's demand to put their armies under Egyptian command. Iraq and the Saudis also placed units under Nasser's command. Crowds hailing Arab unity took to the streets across the Arab world to cheer what they were sure was Palestine's impending liberation. Frantic efforts by the international community were unable to slow the momentum.

Recognizing at last what he had wrought, Nasser made a vain, last-minute attempt to divert the disintegrating situation to a political track. It was too late. On June 5, with the Arabs armies still off balance, Israel launched a preemptive air attack, followed by a lightning strike by its infantry. Within six days, it had defeated all of the assembled forces of its declared enemies. Israeli armies occupied Egypt's Sinai and the Gaza Strip, Syria's Golan Heights, and Jordan's West Bank, including East Jerusalem.

The Arabs were numbed by the debacle. Once again it was *al-nakba,* catastrophe. Nasser proclaimed his readiness to resign his presidency, but, at the demand of the traumatized crowds on Cairo's streets, whose collective life he had dominated for a decade and a half, he consented to stay. Nasserism, however, could not be resuscitated. The dream of Arab nationhood that Nasser had cultivated was dead. Overwhelmed by a sense of humiliating defeat, the Arabs as a people were left once again with devastating uncertainty about where to turn.

VI

THEOCRATS-AUTOCRATS

1968-2005

Arabs had no good explanation for the disaster of 1967 and many took the easy route of blaming the defeat on plots hatched in the West. Egypt, Syria, and Iraq, in retaliation, joined other Arab states in breaking relations with the United States. A few brave thinkers adopted the unpopular position that Arabs should look for the blame within themselves, or at least within their culture. But Arab society, historically resistant to change, is not by nature introspective. Arabs were generally unwilling to upset conventional values, so many of them rooted in history and Islam. The catastrophe produced little in the way of useful insights.

In Syria and Iraq, the Ba'ath regimes tightened their internal controls and narrowed their focus to the local nationalism that Arabs call *al-wataniyya*. Crushing opposition, both slipped into harsh dictatorship. Neither showed a great deal of interest in seeking enlightenment, much less experience, in the outside world. Instead, they hunkered down.

In Egypt, in contrast, the Muslim Brotherhood rose up from the ruins of Nasserism, proclaiming that the poison of secularism, which Pan-Arabism had cultivated throughout Arab society, had to be replaced by a nationalism based on strict religious imperatives. Its arguments fell on sympathetic ears among many Arabs who felt their leaders had erred in deviating from tradition and been seduced by false doctrines.

Meanwhile, the Palestinians, who had long counted on Arab armies to rescue them from Israel's oppression, seethed with contempt for Arab failures. Their loss of confidence in

Arab power generated a new, fierce national consciousness, which was embodied in the Palestine Liberation Organization. If they were to regain their independence, Palestinians concluded, they had to take the responsibility for doing it themselves.

Ironically, it was Nasser who had created the PLO. He had ordered its founding in 1964 within the framework of the Arab League, which he dominated, not so much to free Palestine as to assert his command of the Palestinian cause and, at the same time, to loosen Jordan's rule over the West Bank. Predictably, in early 1967, the PLO's leaders, though beholden to Nasser, joined the widespread Arab clamor provoking him into making war. When the war was over, Nasser no longer controlled the Arab League; nor did Jordan control the West Bank. Into the void stepped a band of audacious young Palestinian nationalists, defying both the Arab establishment and the West. They took over the PLO and vowed to wage the struggle for liberation on their own terms.

Their leader was Yasser Arafat, who had abandoned his training as a civil engineer to serve the Palestinian cause. Arafat, always attentive to his image, claimed descent from an esteemed Jerusalem clan, though evidence sets his birth in 1929 to a rather ordinary Palestinian merchant family living in Cairo. When his mother died a few years later, he was sent to live with relatives in Jerusalem, to which he developed a strong attachment. But he later returned to Cairo, where as a student he mixed prominently in both Egyptian and Palestinian politics.

Records show that, in his student days, Arafat developed an allegiance to Hajj Amin, the militant Palestinian leader, though he actually fought with the Muslim Brothers in 1948 in the war against Israel. Though supportive of Egypt's revolution in 1952, he was jailed several times by Nasser's police, presumably for his Brotherhood ties. Later he made his way to Gaza, where he joined the *fedayeen* in raids across the border, and, though only five feet four and delicately built, he made a reputation as a brave and skillful fighter. In 1957 he first draped a *kouffiya*, his symbol of Arabism, over his balding head. He also broke his ties that year with Egypt, after Nasser, as part of the deal brokered by the United Nations to end the Suez crisis, consented to permit no more raids on Israel from Gaza, effectively suspending the Palestinian armed struggle.

His break with Nasser prompted Arafat to migrate to Kuwait, where, while employed as an engineer, he dedicated himself zealously to political organizing. Having lost faith in Arab arms in 1948 and again at Suez in 1956, he and his friends in Palestine laid plans for a society with liberation as its only ideology. The organization they formed was called Fatah, and it was meant to be independent of all Arab regimes. Fatah's recruits, and most of its financing, were drawn from the community of Palestinian refugees concentrated in the Gulf. Arafat—personally austere, celibate, disorganized but shrewd, a tireless worker, even a compelling fund-raiser—was its leader by consensus. After the 1967 debacle, Nasser was too enfeebled to put up resistance to Fatah's takeover of the PLO.[1]

In an interview with me in 1980, Arafat said:

When our Palestinian movement was founded, we were all excited about Nasser's political revolution, which was then two years old. We were trying to face our tragedy as Palestinians, but we were forbidden to organize ourselves in any way, not only under the Israeli occupation but in the Arab countries, too. Many of us left Cairo to organize underground, inside the occupied territories but also in Iraq, the Gulf, and Saudi Arabia. Everywhere it was forbidden. It was not easy.

The ideology we adopted was then unique in the Arab world. We were not Ba'athis, not Muslim Brothers, not Communists, not Pan-Arab nationalists. We were not part of any existing parties. Fatah's doctrine was purely Palestinian nationalism.

Earlier, we had counted on the Arabs, our brothers, to liberate us. I don't want to say anything bad about them. But I remember being surprised and disappointed when Nasser himself, in 1957, said to a delegation of Palestinians from Gaza, "I don't have any plans to liberate your country, and you should not believe anyone who tells you there is a plan to liberate your country, or to solve the Palestinian question." We founded Fatah to lead the Palestinian movement, because we knew we had to do it ourselves.

The PLO's first model for liberation was Algeria, which had won its independence from France in 1962 after a decade of guerrilla warfare on its own territory. Palestinians had shown no interest in Gandhi's precedent of nonviolence, and, given Israel's ties with the West, conventional diplomacy appeared to them to hold no promise. Algerian-style "armed struggle"—liberation through "the barrel of a gun"—seemed a logical course. Yet, in practice, the PLO was unable to match the Algerians in rallying its people to rise up against foreign occupation. After a few years of negligible results, the PLO had to search for a different strategy.

The revised strategy was to adapt guerrilla warfare to a global battlefield. The result was that, throughout the 1970s, the PLO received a huge amount of attention from hijackings, bombings, and assassinations, conducted not just against Israel but against the West as a whole. Its actions kept Palestine liberation on the international agenda, which was itself a victory, but they won the PLO few friends and no territory. The PLO's operations reached a climax in the murder in 1972 of a dozen Israeli athletes at the Olympic Games in Munich. The widespread disgust that the killings engendered cast doubt even among Palestinians about whether such brutality advanced their cause.

In parallel, the PLO followed a course aimed at expanding its power base into Palestine's neighbor states. Notwithstanding the sovereignty of these states, it was quite willing to impose Palestinian over Arab interests. The PLO seized control of the seething refugee camps within Jordan and Lebanon, where hundreds of thousands of Palestinians lived, waiting in vain to return home. It made them into armed fortresses. In the wake of the 1967 defeat, when the governments of Jordan and Lebanon acknowledged that it was pointless to stir up the Israelis, neither was able to stop the provocations of the PLO, which kept their borders in constant turmoil.

The PLO, in fact, took aim at the sovereignty of both states. A showdown with Jordan came in September 1970—known to Arabs as Black September—after a radical wing within the PLO hijacked four Western airliners, landing three of them at a remote Jordanian airport. Arafat seized command of the operation and secured the release of the passengers, but the PLO blew up the planes. King Hussein, his authority in doubt in his own land, at one point seemed ready to bow to Arafat by abdicating, which would have left Jordan in the PLO's hands. But the king stiffened and, turning his army loose, transformed what had been sporadic Jordanian resistance to Palestinian forces into a resolute defense of the kingdom.

With Arabs killing Arabs, the fighting threatened to engulf the entire region. The Ba'ath regimes of Syria and Iraq, seeing the opportunity to unseat the Jordanian king, mobilized to reinforce the PLO. In response, the U.S. fleet in the Mediterranean and the Israeli air force went on full alert, sending a clear message of support as Jordan's army moved into position to stop a Syrian column headed for Amman. The Syrians

retreated and Arafat, after heavy Palestinian losses, acknowledged the futility of fighting on. By early 1971, the PLO's
forces in Jordan had either laid down their arms or fled to
Lebanon.

In Lebanon, the PLO had equally grand designs. In the
decades after the 1948 war, the Palestinians living in the misery of the refugee camps there had taken care not to disturb
the fragile balance among Lebanon's ethnic groups. But in the
aftermath of Black September, the PLO remade these camps
into bases from which it attacked Israel and imposed its influence throughout Lebanon's south. Heavily Shi'ite, the region
became known as Fatahland, but the PLO's ambitions, along
with its ceaseless raids on Israel, generated a crisis that spread
throughout the country.

Israel's strategy of retaliating fiercely, without distinguish-
ing between Palestinians and Lebanese, split Lebanon between PLO sympathizers, most of them Muslim, and PLO
antagonists, mostly Christian. The disruptions also fanned
grievances that had simmered among Lebanese since the National Pact of 1943. Civil war broke out in 1975, and though
Palestinians had little stake in its outcome, Arafat could not
undo the damage the PLO had done.

Tens of thousands died in the war, not just Christian, Druze,
and Muslim Lebanese, but Palestinians caught in the cross fire.
Syria dispatched an occupying army to contain the carnage,
but the fighting reached a level that threatened the equlibrium
of the Arab world itself. It ended only in 1989, when the Arab
League convoked a meeting of the exhausted belligerents in
Taif, Saudi Arabia, where they reached an accord based largely
on a reaffirmation of the prewar status quo.

Even as the blood flowed, Arafat persevered in his border
attacks on Israel. In 1982, after years of retaliatory raiding, Israel moved up to a full-scale invasion of Lebanon. Inevitably
it complicated Lebanon's internecine conflict but its aim was

to crush PLO military power once and for all. Advancing far beyond the PLO camps in the south, Israel drove the Palestinian forces into a redoubt in Beirut. While the Syrians stood by watching, the PLO fought bravely, but it was overmatched. Under terms negotiated by U.S. diplomats between the Palestinians and Israelis, the PLO's besieged forces in Beirut set sail for Tunis, where Arafat relocated his headquarters, farther from the homeland than ever.

Even Arafat knew that the invasion ended the PLO's dream of victory by "armed struggle." But it also produced some surprises. The PLO's defeat had not crushed the spirit of Palestinian resistance itself, as the popular uprising in the West Bank and Gaza, known as the *intifada,* would soon show. It had also turned around the Shi'ites of southern Lebanon, who became the enemies of Israel's occupation once the PLO departed. But the wars in Lebanon, like the showdown in Jordan, had demonstrated the limits of the PLO's military power, and imposed once again the need to shift to a new liberation strategy.

The initiative, this time, did not come from Arafat. At the end of 1987, the stone-throwing practices of Arab boys in the occupied territories, symbolic acts of resistance, exploded into the first insurgency since Israel's conquest twenty years earlier. Insofar as it had leaders, the *intifada* was led by a new generation, products of the refugee camps who had lived their entire lives under Israeli guns. They surprised their own elders, but they also surprised Arafat, who, from Tunis, tried to bring them under his control. And they surprised the Israelis, who had become complacent about resistance and had no plan for ending it. The *intifada* imposed on Israel the recognition that the enemy now was not just a collection of weak Arab states and a terrorist organization of limited capacity but the 3 million Palestinians who lived within the perimeters of its own military control.

The response of Israelis to Palestinian resistance was—and remains—divided. A movement of settlers had dug its roots into the soil of the occupied territories and intended to remain there. The settlers regarded the victory of 1967 as a mandate for a Greater Israel and demanded intensified military action to suppress the local population. But a growing number of Israelis saw the *intifada* as evidence that it was time for the two peoples to reach a deal.

Many Palestinians were moving in the same direction. As early as 1970, some talked openly of reexamining the partition proposal first made in the Peel report of 1937. Since then, partition had remained on the international agenda. After the 1967 war, the partition formula was rewritten at the United Nations in the form of Security Council Resolution 242, which called for the exchange of land for peace. In 1974 Arafat himself signaled a reconsideration of his earlier intransigence by announcing to the General Assembly that the PLO would settle in Palestine for "a little homeland of our own."

In the 1980s, the Palestine National Council, an assortment of delegates meeting as a parliament in exile, went on record in favor of a Palestinian state in the West Bank and the Gaza Strip. Within the PLO, the contest among factions over partition continued to be vehement—in fact, it took a few lives—leaving outsiders unclear over the real policy. Meanwhile, Palestinian heirs of the Muslim Brothers, notably the newly organized Hamas, reasserted the Islamic objection to any Jewish state at all. Nonetheless, in the 1990s terms of the Arab-Israeli debate steadily shifted. Even the vocabulary changed, as influential Palestinians joined compromise-oriented Israelis in groping for a consensus on a "two-state solution."

The move toward a two-state solution took a leap forward under the Oslo Accord of 1993, when Arafat shook hands with Israeli prime minister Yitzhak Rabin under the gaze of U.S. president Bill Clinton on the White House lawn. Israel consented to limited self-rule by the Palestinians in the occupied territories in return for an end of violence. But progress toward implementation came to a halt in 1995 when Rabin was assassinated by an ultra-orthodox antipeace zealot. In July 2000, Clinton initiated a resumption of negotiations, with Arafat and Ehud Barak, Israel's leader, at Camp David, Maryland. The talks collapsed, with each side blaming the other for the failure. Soon thereafter, Clinton surrendered the presidency to George W. Bush, while Barak gave way to Ariel Sharon, neither of whom showed an interest in serious bargaining.

The breakdown of Clinton's talks at Camp David ignited a second *intifada*, far more lethal than the first. Israel responded by reoccupying the cities it had vacated under the Oslo Accord and by isolating Arafat in his headquarters in the West Bank town of Ramallah. Intracommunal carnage was heavier than it had been since the war for Israel's independence in 1948. The Palestinian weapon of choice was the suicide bomb; the Israelis retaliated with planes and tanks. Each side was outraged by the other's arms, and its selection of victims. Between 2000 and 2005, roughly three thousand Palestinians and one thousand Israelis were killed, while the material destruction in the Palestinian areas was enormous.

Arafat, after a brief illness, died in November 2004, when prospects for a resolution of the Palestinian conflict appeared to be at a nadir. Insiders and outsiders alike expressed hope that the change in Palestinian leadership would favor agreement. Indeed, Mahmoud Abbas, Arafat's successor, was a longtime PLO official who had openly advocated negotiation over conflict. By now, both Israel and the Palestinian Authority, successor to the PLO, had joined the United States in endorsing the principle of the two-state solution. Ostensibly, the gap between the two sides was narrowing, especially after Prime Minister Sharon withdrew Israeli settlements from the Gaza Strip. But President Bush remained passive as an intermediary, and the terms both sides set seemed to leave a settlement as distant as ever.

———

In September 1970, Gamal Abdul Nasser died of a massive heart attack and was succeeded by Anwar Sadat, his vice president. Sadat's vision of Egypt's future was very different from Nasser's. Born, like Nasser, in a village in the Nile Delta, he moved with his family to Cairo after his father joined a government ministry. When the British expanded the Egyptian army on the eve of World War II, both Sadat and Nasser seized the chance to climb the social ladder by entering the military academy. More political than most of his circle, Sadat preceded and may even have recruited Nasser into the Free Officers. Later, as Nasser's vice president, he was lightly regarded, and his break from Nasser's course revealed a daring that astonished both Egypt and the outside world.[2]

As president, Sadat, though hardly a democrat, polished the harsher edges of Nasser's despotism. More important, however, he vowed to lift the burdens on Egypt of recurring wars by turning Nasser's nationalism upside down. He saw his predecessor's Pan-Arabism as a negation of Egypt's nationhood, which to him dated back to the Pharaohs' time. Sadat considered Egypt different from the Arab world, and regaining the Sinai more important than retaining a spiritual bond with the *umma*. In making overtures to Israel, he shattered the Arab world's united front. His willingness to reach a settlement with the Jewish state made him the Arabs' most controversial leader, and probably their most despised.

Naguib Mahfouz, who shared Sadat's notion of Egypt's Pharaonic roots, took pride in having been among the few Egyptian thinkers who, well before Sadat, had talked about making peace with Israel. Occasionally, this view even invaded his writing, though obliquely. No one in his group of friends, he said, was bold enough to openly advocate peace.

"I witnessed five wars in my generation," he told me, "and after every one we had to start from zero to rebuild the country. Sadat and Nasser both knew we could not wage another war against Israel. So why not peace? In a few of my articles I said we had to leave our dreamworld and concentrate on development. The Arabs didn't like it when I suggested spending money on culture rather than arms. I did not share the popular belief that peace with Israel would destroy the self-esteem of the Arab people."

On July 18, 1972, Sadat astounded the world by expelling the fifteen thousand Russians who constituted the backbone of Egypt's military establishment. In dramatic fashion, the move severed the bond with the Soviet Union that Nasser had initiated in 1955. If Sadat's objective was to coax Washington away from its support of Israel, however, he failed. America, under Richard Nixon, proposed no peace negotiations. Raising his offer, Sadat proposed to rebuild Egypt's cities along the Suez Canal—in effect, making them hostages to peace—in return for Israel's retreat from the canal's banks. When Israel declined, Washington raised no objection, and the opportunity was lost. Measured from the perspective of 1972, Sadat's overtures did nothing to break the Middle East deadlock.

But on the morning of the Jewish holy day of Yom Kippur in 1973, Sadat broke the deadlock on his own. Egypt's army, taking Israel by surprise, crossed the Suez Canal, pierced the Israeli defenses, and advanced into the Sinai. At the same time, the Syrians fell on the Israeli forces in the north with a massive tank offensive across the Golan Heights. Israeli strategic doctrine had held that the Arabs were incapable of such assaults. The Yom Kippur attack was by far their most powerful and skillful military undertaking. Though its objective was limited to redressing the Arabs' negotiating inferiority, Sadat's attack was so successful that in its first days many Israelis feared for the existence of the state itself.

This was the war in which the Arabs imposed an oil embargo on the West, a weapon that was far more powerful than their armies. Sadat had devised the strategy with the Saudis, whose dominance of the market had recently been affirmed by a sharp fall in available American oil. With prices rising, Arab producers could cut back on oil deliveries without reducing their total income. The embargo imposed gasoline shortages while fear of economic paralysis spread through the industrial world. For the first time Washington was forced to consider modifying its support of Israel.

Curiously, it was Sadat who called the embargo off. As he saw it, shifting the regional balance of power from Israel to the Arabs was less important than ending Egypt's wars, which he regarded as dependent on Washington's stepping into the diplomatic breach. Thanks to Sadat, the embargo never attained strategic potential; moreover, the Arabs have never used the weapon again.[3]

On the battlefield, the United States responded slowly to Israel's initial reverses, but in the second week it began the delivery of supplies that helped turn the fighting around. By that time, the two superpowers had folded the conflict into the Cold War, with each heavily resupplying its own client. To avoid stumbling into conflict themselves, however, they decided in the third week of the war to impose a cease-fire, and to have the United Nations reaffirm in Resolution 338 the principle, first stated after the 1967 war, of exchanging land for peace. The losses on both sides were severe: more than twelve thousand Arabs, nearly three thousand Israelis. In the end Israel was victorious, but in committing America to action in favor of an Egpytian-Israeli political settlement, Sadat achieved his goal.

In January 1974, Secretary of State Henry Kissinger, who had rejected Sadat's peace overture two years earlier, produced over the course of a week of "shuttle diplomacy" an agreement to separate the two hostile armies that stood nose to nose in the Sinai Desert. The deal provided for Israel's first evacuation—and the Arabs' first reoccupation—of land captured in 1967. Egypt, in return, pledged to reopen the Suez Canal and rebuild the cities along its banks. The agreement was a major step forward not just in restoring Egyptian territory but in relieving the paralysis in Arab-Israeli relations.

An Israeli-Syrian agreement, next on Kissinger's agenda, proved harder to achieve, however. Syria's resentment of Palestine's loss under the Sykes-Picot Agreement had scarcely abated. In contention between the two states was the Golan Heights, which Israel held as a strategic buffer, but which Syria coveted as land that had been cultivated by Syrians throughout history. With both sides holding out, the PLO aggravated tensions with a series of deadly raids from Lebanon. One of them killed twenty-four children in the border town of Ma'alot. It took thirty-four days of contentious bargaining before Washington came up with a formula the two parties would accept. Contrary to expectations, it has kept the peace on the Israel-Syrian frontier ever since.

The Israeli-Syrian accord gave Kissinger reason to believe that if he acted decisively, the United States might squeeze Moscow out of the region altogether. Israel, however, did not share this priority. It rejected not only another deal with Sadat but, even more firmly, Kissinger's proposals for negotiations with Jordan and a second round with Syria. Israel's policy was no doubt influenced by rising pressure from the Israeli settlers' movement to retain the occupied territories, particularly Jordan's West Bank, as part of a Greater Israel. But Sadat would not be denied, and Kissinger supported his determination to get back all of the Sinai.

After arduous bargaining, Israel and Egypt reached a second agreement. Israel withdrew farther into the Sinai, even returning Egypt's oil fields. Sadat, for his part, consented to demilitarize the evacuated area. What was more important, Israel obtained a monumental commitment from the United States: to guarantee its military superiority, free from supervision, over the Arab world. Called Sinai II, the accord—since absorbed into America's strategic calculations in the Middle East—offered Israel the assurance that it would remain the region's strongest military power, with no need to make further territorial concessions.

Since Israel had no incentive to bargain further, Sinai II was followed by a negotiating stalemate, and to break it Sadat made his celebrated visit to Jerusalem in November 1977. In a dramatic speech to the Israeli Knesset, he declared that his goal was not just an Egyptian-Israeli settlement but a comprehensive peace, which included an end to occupation of the Palestinians. He called it Egypt's moral duty. He also promised that Israel, as part of a comprehensive peace, would be welcomed into the community of Middle East nations.

In the wake of Sadat's visit, the psychological barriers between Israelis and Arabs tottered, but they did not tumble. Though Israelis exulted in the prospect of acceptance, they had recently elected a right-wing government that opposed giving up territory at all. In 1979, after two years of negotiations led by U.S. president Jimmy Carter, Israel and Egypt finally signed a treaty, which was a huge achievement, but it fell short of Sadat's promise to liberate the Palestinians. Sadat signed an *Egyptian* peace, far from the comprehensive Arab-Israeli peace he had vowed. It left the Palestinians still under Israeli rule, a situation that nearly all Arabs found unaccept-

able. It was a peace that left Israel and the Arab world effectively still at war.

Sadat, Naguib Mahfouz told me, "was a man who did great
things, but who also made big mistakes. . . . Nasser considered
himself a god, but Sadat thought he was a Pharaoh. . . . He
moved us back toward democracy but far from real democracy. It was controlled and disciplined, and it retained authoritarian traces. But it was a change of direction which, with
some setbacks, has continued. Sadat's great contribution was
to turn the country to constructive goals and values. The most
important was to bring Egypt peace."

But two and a half years later, Sadat was killed in a hail of
bullets fired by a ring of Islamic nationalists concealed within
Egypt's army. His assassins, legatees of the Muslim Brotherhood's Hassan al-Banna, claimed the name Islamic Jihad.
They reproached Sadat for apostasy, and for the peace he
made with Israel. Ironically, they gunned him down as he re-
viewed a parade celebrating the anniversary of Egypt's greatest military triumph over Israel, crossing the Suez Canal.

Indirectly, Sadat had himself helped germinate the plot.
In contrast to Nasser's harsh suppression, Sadat endorsed
the Muslim Brotherhood's rehabilitation. Though worldly in
many ways, Sadat was a practicing Muslim who had flirted
with the brotherhood in his youth. He liked to call himself the
"believer-president." In proposing to restore the brotherhood
to Egypt's political mainstream, he calculated that it would
counter the secular Nasserists who opposed his peace policies. It was a serious mistake. The Brothers, once back in business, not only objected to the peace with Israel but harassed
students and Christians, and sought to impose a religious uni-
formity on Egyptian society. Moreover, in their refusal to tol-
erate any reconciliation with the West, they were far more
radical than Nasser's followers had ever been.

"I utterly reject that the assassination was a popular repudiation of Sadat's policy of peace," Mahfouz went on. "I was there the day Sadat returned from Israel in 1977. Five million people showed up, and their enthusiasm was genuine. There was no doubt they were ready for peace. Sadat's killers were an exception among Egyptians. They considered him an apostate, and they thought killing him was Islam's big chance to seize power. Egyptians were disappointed not by peace but only by what the peace failed to deliver—a settlement for the Palestinians and prosperity at home. I know of no one who regretted that we were at peace."

Mahfouz may have exaggerated the popular fervor for peace. In contrast to the mass mourning for Nasser, few tears were shed at the death of Sadat. In part, the explanation was personal: Nasser, whatever his faults, was direct, earthy, and honest, while Sadat, who extolled his peasant origins but lived opulently, was perceived as a hypocrite. Mahfouz, however, was correct about popular remorse over the Palestinians. Even Egyptians who favored peace felt that the *separate* peace to which Sadat had agreed violated their moral obligations as Arabs and as Muslims. Many, refusing reconciliation with Israel without Palestinian freedom, feel the same today.

———

Sadat's murder in 1981 was a milestone in the rise of radical Islamic nationalism. One can question whether Islamic radicalism would have emerged at all had Nasser not so thoroughly discredited Pan-Arabism. At the least, Nasser's failures created an ideological void into which Islamic radicalism poured. For more than a decade after the 1967 debacle, religious radicalism rose incrementally among Arabs, but then huge Islamic waves broke in distant Iran and Afghanistan. Sadat's assassination signaled that the waters had reached the Arab world and that an Islamic flood was beginning to inundate the Middle East.

The wave from Iran came first. In February 1979, Ayatollah Ruhollah Khomeini returned from exile to seize control of a revolution that had overthrown the despotic shah, Muhammad Reza Pahlavi. Khomeini announced the founding of a state based on the laws of Shi'a Islam. But the roots of the Khomeini revolution, like those of Arab nationalism, lay in a deep-seated popular resentment of Western colonialism.

Those roots had sprouted in the proto-protectorate that Britain imposed after World War I, when it took over Iran's army and treasury while controlling the oil company that was the source of Iran's rising wealth. In 1951, a democratically elected government under Muhammad Mosaddiq proposed to nationalize the oil company; Britain and the United States retaliated by imposing an economic embargo. For Washington, the stakes had to do not with money but with the Cold War. The United States regarded Mosaddiq as sympathetic to Moscow, and with assistance from the CIA, royalists in Iran's army overthrew him in August 1953. During the turmoil, the shah fled into exile, only to return a few days later under the protection of the United States. Over the ensuing decades, the shah's regime grew increasingly despotic; in the eyes of most Iranians, America was the force behind the despotism.

Though the shah was opposed by democrats and liberals in Iran, in the years after the Mosaddiq coup Khomeini's Islamic movement emerged as his most dangerous foe. In 1964 the shah expelled Khomeini to Najaf, the Shi'ite holy city in neighboring Iraq. But with Khomeini agitating through a secret network of agents and propagandists, the shah's popular support went into sharp decline. In the 1970s, Tehran's streets were the scene of massive strikes. The shah issued desperate pleas to Washington to help; in exile, Khomeini cited these pleas as proof that the shah was America's lackey. Under President Jimmy Carter, the United States failed to come to the shah's rescue.

In 1978, with the fervor in Iran enflaming the Shi'ites in Iraq, Saddam Hussein expelled Khomeini from Najaf, but the expulsion did not slow his momentum. Following a detour in France, Khomeini arrived in Tehran in triumph, two weeks after the shah's abdication. The concept of an Islamic state, with which Khomeini returned, alarmed secular Iranians, even religious moderates. But Khomeini was so acclaimed that, in a referendum, voters endorsed his Islamic constitution almost unanimously.

Iran's revolution was a repudiation not just of the shah but of America, where the shah took refuge after Tehran. When the United States refused the shah's extradition, Khomeini declared the American embassy a "nest of spies," inciting student militants to invade it. The embassy's capture and the holding of fifty-two hostages—not released until Carter's administration was replaced by Ronald Reagan's 444 days later—was a humiliation for America, further embittering what Khomeini had taken to terming a contest between Satan and God.

The embassy's capture permitted Khomeini to boast to the faithful that Islam had the power to defeat any enemy, even America itself. Khomeini's success demonstrated to the growing Islamic nationalist movement outside Iran, especially in the Arab world, that the goal of a *shari'a* state was attainable.

Meanwhile, inside Iran the revolution turned increasingly bloody. Even while claiming moral superiority, Khomeini showed himself the shah's equal in brutality. He executed thousands whom he judged loyal to the old regime, and when a pro-Communist faction turned on him, he slaughtered thousands more. Later, he decided to "export" the revolution, and imposed no limit on the cost he was willing to accept in human lives.

Iran's neighbor Iraq traced its hostility to Khomeini back to the historic rivalry between ancient empires. Saddam characterized the revolution as a Persian plot against Arab nationalism, as well as a Shi'ite attack on Sunni Islam. He feared, with reason, that Khomeini would subvert the loyalty of Iraqi Shi'ites, a majority of Iraq's population.

Iraq and Iran, whatever the contrast in form, were now alike in being aggressively nationalistic. Iraq's Ba'athis had adopted a secular model, aspiring to a Western-style industrial society. Saddam, abandoning the Pan-Arabism in Ba'ath ideology, sought to lead a rebirth of Arab power. Khomeini's constitution aimed at an Arab audience in declaring the revolution's goal to be "the happiness, under Islam, of all human beings." Khomeini openly declared his intention of "exporting the revolution" and called Iran "the starting point" for Islam's worldwide spread. A collision of the two regimes was inevitable.

Khomeini threw down the gauntlet by repudiating a 1975 treaty in which the two states pledged noninterference in each other's affairs, but in September 1980, Iraq took the initiative in invading Iran. Iraq's ill-equipped forces, initially successful, quickly ground to a halt. Iran counterattacked the next spring, clearing the enemy from the homeland. With higher morale and triple the population, Iran seemed to be a heavy favorite in the contest.

But, despite annual offenses with huge armies, Iran advanced no further. To Khomeini's dismay, Iraq's Shi'ites declined his entreaties to join him as allies. Iraq several times offered a truce, which Khomeini rejected with contempt, vowing to fight until Saddam fell and Iraq adopted an Islamic regime. So for eight bloody years the two armies went at each other, with Iraq and possibly Iran using chemical weapons. As many as a million men died on the battlefield.

America, without much fondness for Saddam, made an early judgment that Khomeini was the more dangerous of the two. With occasional hedging, notably during the "Irangate" scandal when it sent arms to Iran, it provided major assistance to Iraq in intelligence and logistics. These war years were the high point of American-Iraqi relations. In 1988, with Iraq's forces near exhaustion, America's own naval forces intervened, inflicting serious damage against Iran in the waters of the Gulf. The intervention, in combination with an international boycott that seriously disrupted the Iranian economy, forced the ayatollah to give in.

To Khomeini, bowing to Washington was slightly less painful than bowing to Saddam, whom he had never forgiven for expelling him from Najaf. Still, Khomeini described the cease-fire as "worse than taking poison." A year later he died, and Iran seemed to lose much of its fervor for spreading the revolution. Though the Islamic state has survived without serious domestic opposition, its popularity has probably declined. Outside Iran, however, the Islamic nationalism that Khomeini represented has surged. Iran passed to the Arabs the fire of its revolution, along with the example of establishing Islamic rule. In doing so, Khomeini honed the edge of the Arabs' long-standing animosity toward the West.

———

Afghanistan, Iran's neighbor to the east, exploded within months of Khomeini's victory in 1979, climaxing a turbulent decade during which regimes followed one after another in Kabul, the capital. Though overwhelmingly Islamic, Afghanistan was riven by hostile ethnic groups, many under warlords commanding substantial militias. Stirring up this volatile mix were organizations of pro-Communists and Islamic nationalists. A pro-Soviet military cabal seized power in 1978, but its ongoing weakness, despite Moscow's help, made its survival uncertain. The next year, Russia, vowing to restore order on its frontier, invaded Afghanistan, giving its mutually hostile sects a reason to coalesce. Temporarily united, they presented the Soviet Union with far more resistance than it could possibly have expected.

Long isolated, Afghanistan suddenly became an arena in the Cold War. America's expulsion from Iran had intensified its anxieties over the future of Central Asia. As a companion to the Eisenhower Doctrine, it had proclaimed the Carter Doctrine to warn the USSR of its readiness to fight to preserve its interests. Though Washington did not regard the Afghan factions as capable of winning the war, it decided to help them with money and arms, hoping to keep Russia off balance and discourage it from further mischief.

The U.S. commitment created an incongruous bond. Islamic nationalists from around the world mobilized in Afghanistan to defend the faith against Soviet atheism. Thousands of them—called *mujahidin,* holy warriors—flocked to training camps, where they deepened their religious beliefs before going into battle alongside the local militias. Though not quite admitting the United States as their ally, they gladly accepted American weapons, bringing a temporary lull to the anti-American vituperation that had by now become intrinsic to Arab nationalism.

Still, few had anticipated the outcome of the Afghan war. Thanks in large part to the United States, the Afghan coalition emerged victorious against the USSR, and, in December 1989, the defeated Russians withdrew from the country. More astonishingly, a few months later the regime in Moscow itself collapsed.[4] The Cold War was over, realigning relations among many nations of the world. But between the Arab states and the West, the old animosities quickly reappeared. The passing of the Cold War may even have intensified them.

The Cold War's termination, eliminating the Russian factor in strategic calculations, suddenly placed the Arab states in a direct confrontation with America. Britain and France had receded, since Suez, as objects of Arab animosity. Having won the East-West conflict, the United States appeared invulnerable; inevitably, it would become subject to the temptations of uncontested power. The United States took the place of the old colonial states to become the unique target of the Arabs' anti-Western grievances. In its new position, the United States served as a springboard to bring together Arab nationalism's religious and secular wings.

In Afghanistan, the old problems intensified after the Russians left. The United States lost interest in the Afghans, opening the door even wider to Islamic radicalism. The familiar ethnic quarrels resumed, and America's leftover arms made them deadlier than ever. But the old militias crumbled before the military offensive of a new radical army, called the Taliban, or "students." The Taliban's recruits had emerged from the *madrassas,* Islamic academies heavily supported by the Saudis, of the wartime training camps. By the mid-1990s, the Taliban ruled most of Afghanistan, and wherever they took over, they issued decrees that required men to wear turbans and beards and to pray five times daily, women to remain indoors and to cover themselves with all-concealing *burqas.* The absence of popular protest against the Taliban's stern rule suggested that, after the years of violence, Afghans were simply grateful for the respite.[5]

The Taliban, however, were only one agent of the Islamic radicalization produced by the Afghan war. The young believers, most of them Arabs, who had flocked to the Afghan resistance during the 1980s were to have an impact of their own. Like the Taliban's, their training included the *madrassas,* where they were exposed to the zealotry of Saudi Wahhabism. After their tours fighting the Soviets, thousands of them fanned out across the Muslim world. Their influence as missionaries of religious extremism surpassed the Taliban's, especially in the Arab world.

The "Afghans," as they were called, became an arm of the anti-Western militance introduced into Islam by the Muslim Brotherhood decades before. They conveyed their influence in the schools, the bureaucracies, and the courts. They helped transform the street scene in great cities like Cairo, which, after decades of growing cosmopolitanism, retreated to strict Islamic conservatism. Anwar Sadat's murder was evidence that the Afghans also injected into the mainstream of Arab political life a strong disposition to violence.

Most dramatically, the Afghan war produced Osama bin Laden, the apostle of global terror. Scion of a prominent Saudi family, he had put his life and substantial fortune on the line to fight "Soviet atheism." But his core beliefs went deeper, to the conviction that the duty of Muslims lay in combat, in *jihad,* to resume Islam's historic struggle against Christian power. Once the USSR fell, his principal enemy became the West. Inside Afghanistan, bin Laden organized al-Qaeda to undertake global missions. The Taliban, when they took over the country, provided him with a sanctuary for its training and operations. Though bin Laden attracted little international notice in the 1990s, that was soon to change.[6]

Among other consequences of the Soviet Union's collapse was the opportunity it offered to Washington to reconsider its Persian Gulf strategy. Until the 1960s, the United States had relied on British imperial forces to safeguard Western oil interests. America's own Gulf flotilla—based at a modest facility in Bahrain—did little more than show the flag. As long as the Cold War lasted, the two superpowers, wary of provoking each other, had stayed clear of the Gulf, leaving a vacuum of power there. The only military force available to America to keep an eye on the region was Iran, its surrogate. When the shah fell, U.S. military capacity in the Gulf all but vanished. The Soviet collapse a decade later, however, offered another dramatic reversal. It meant Washington had acquired a free hand in the Gulf, the world's richest reservoir of oil.

But in the decade between the shah's fall and the Soviet collapse, Saudi Arabia became America's fallback power. America's involvement with the Saudis dated back to World War II, when President Franklin Roosevelt declared the nation strategically important, thus eligible for lend-lease. In 1945 Roosevelt held a celebrated shipboard meeting with the Saudi king, Abdul Aziz, placing a symbolic seal on the friendship. Oil was Roosevelt's principal but not his only concern. Late in the war, the United States built an airfield at Dahran, in eastern Saudi Arabia, which developed in subsequent years into a military asset that permitted American planes to reach deep into Soviet Asia.

After World War II, President Truman went a step further, designating the kingdom a recipient of American military training and equipment. As petrodollars poured in, the Saudis deposited tens of billions through purchases and investments into the coffers of American finance and industry. In the 1950s, when Nasserism was sweeping through the Arab world, the Saudi government stood reliably at America's side. In large measure, its position during the Nasser era was the product of inter-Arab rivalry, but it emerged also from the royal family's deep, religiously based aversion to the atheism inherent in Soviet Communism.[7]

Yet the Saudis' religion—the puritanical Wahhabi Islam—also made the United States uneasy. The Sauds, unaccountable tribal despots, spent colossal sums not just on themselves but on mosques and *madrassas* across the Muslim world, promoting a version of the faith that was inherently hostile to the West. Though the Saud family had won its sovereignty over Arabia on its own, making it virtually alone among Arab rulers without debts to the West, many Saudis were uneasy with the intimate ties it later established with the infidels. In its obsession with Communism, Washington chose to over-look the possibility that Wahhabism might in its own way also be dangerous. Even after Iran's revolution introduced the West to the perils of Islamic extremism, the United States professed to see little in common between Khomeini's theology and the Sauds'.

Then, in November 1979, during the annual *hajj*, some 250 heavily armed Islamic warriors seized the Great Mosque in Mecca and took thousands of pilgrims hostage. Though they were Saudi fanatics, Sunnis without an obvious link to Shi'ite Iran, they were clearly inspired by Khomeini. The United States, which had long expected democratic reform in Saudi Arabia, was shocked at a popular insurgency, based on *jihad*, whose aim was to push the society back to Islam's origins. The attackers denounced the royal family's lack of Islamic rigor, its relations with America, its extravagant lifestyle. The Sauds emerged victorious after weeks of bloody combat; they ended the struggle with a flourish by publicly beheading sixty-three of the rebels. But the incident forced the royal family to recognize its vulnerability and to embrace an even more conspicuous Islamic piety.

Washington, notwithstanding, saw no choice but to support the Sauds, the only candidates available to fill the opening left by the shah. It was not that Saudi Arabia had much military potential, despite years of huge military expenditures. When in Riyadh once, I asked Prince Saud al-Faisal, the foreign minister, why his country's army was so much weaker than Israel's, despite a rough equivalence in population. He bristled at the comparison, muttering blandly, "Building an army takes time. . . . We have to develop our human resources." But Saudi officials, when pressed, admitted that the royal family had no appetite—particularly after the Mecca insurgency—for developing a standing army that might one day turn against it, and preferred to rely on America for its security.

Given what was at stake in the oil fields, the United States accepted the responsibility, and over the 1980s its relationship with the Sauds grew stronger.

As the 1990s began, with the Soviet Union out of the picture, Saddam Hussein represented the only challenge to America's hegemony in the Gulf. His success in containing Iran's revolution had swelled his sense of himself and of his power. His propaganda, emphasizing an Iraqi heritage going back to ancient Babylon, conveyed an imperial vision. Iraq's oil wealth, second only to the Saudis', offered a foundation for his dream of grandeur. At the least, Saddam wanted the world to respect him as preeminent in the Gulf, a conception starkly at odds with Washington's.

After Saddam's victory over Khomeini in 1988, neither he nor America made much effort to preserve the friendly ties they had cultivated during the war. Iraq's cease-fire with Iran was followed by two years of mutual testiness between Washington and Baghdad. It reached a climax in a dispute that Saddam provoked over Iraq's war debt to Kuwait.

Like Saudi Arabia, Kuwait had feared the threat Khomeini posed and supported Saddam's decision in 1980 to invade Iran. Saddam argued quite persuasively that all or part of the debt should be forgiven in consideration of the blood Iraq had spilled to protect Kuwait. But Kuwait gave no ground. To Washington, Kuwait was a vital link in its emerging Gulf security system, a buffer against aggression by either Iraq or Iran against America's clients the Sauds. During the Iraq-Iran war, the United States had pledged to protect Kuwait, presumably against Khomeini. Saddam seemed convinced that the pledge no longer applied.

Saddam's army seized Kuwait in August 1990 and, according to some U.S. analysts, was poised to advance into Saudi Arabia. U.S. intelligence photos left some doubt about whether this was Saddam's intention, but with America prepared to act against him, the Saudis were not disposed to take a chance. By depicting Saddam as the embodiment of evil, President George H. W. Bush, father of the later incumbent, saw no need to explain his policy within the context of America's Persian Gulf strategy.

Bush organized a Western coalition, which was joined by Egypt and Syria as well as by Saudi Arabia, Arab states that rejected Saddam's transgression against a sovereign Kuwait. Saddam's well-worn anti-Western and anti-Israeli slogans, along with calls for patience from a few Arab leaders, changed no minds. According to some reports, Osama bin Laden offered the Saudi government an army of 100,000 holy warriors to liberate Kuwait on the condition it keep out infidel troops, but the royal family declined the offer.[8]

In February 1991, a coalition army of 500,000 Western and Arab soldiers, operating with United Nations endorsement from Saudi bases, assaulted Kuwait. The Iraqis, outmatched in numbers, equipment, and technology, were quickly routed. But Washington—in a curious reprise of its rescue of Nasser from defeat at Suez in 1956—decided not to bring Saddam down. President Bush claimed the coalition's UN mandate did not permit its pursuit of Iraq's army. Instead, America opted for a policy of undermining Iraq from afar. In allowing Saddam to escape, the United States enabled him to remain in power for another decade.

In its endgame to the Gulf war of 1991, America provided cover to the Kurds in Iraq's north to establish an autonomous regime. In the south, in contrast, it encouraged a Shi'ite uprising, then did nothing to stop Saddam from crushing it. Throughout the 1990s, U.S. planes periodically bombed cities and military installations in Iraq. With UN authorization, the United States also enforced a rigorous economic embargo.

Without jeopardizing the Saddam regime's survival, the U.S. siege of Iraq gave Iraqis cause to blame America for years of misery in their daily lives.

Saddam, after his Kuwait fiasco, grew increasingly despotic. He tolerated no dissent and retaliated against any hint of domestic opposition with executions, torture, and imprisonment. My own observation on trips to Iraq in this period was that the Iraqis who had once admired his leadership, not just in fighting the war with Iran but in his work in the prewar years to develop a modern state, came increasingly to detest him. Yet through his tyrannical practices, and by effectively administering a program that kept Iraqis clothed and fed, he managed to defeat the American embargo and preserve his power. Then in 2001 George W. Bush assumed the American presidency, solemnly vowing "regime change."

—

Osama bin Laden, meanwhile, was ratcheting up his *jihad*. He left no doubt, as an Islamic nationalist, that America was his enemy, as it was Saddam's. But Saddam ran a secular regime, and even during the decade of the siege, the theocratic bin Laden gave him no backing. Though bin Laden decried America's support of Israel, he poured more of his vitriol on the Saudi monarchy for allowing American military bases on Islam's sacred soil. Bin Laden's religious nationalism emerges in a celebrated *fatwa:*

> The Arabian Peninsula has never been stormed by any forces like the crusader armies spreading in it like locusts, eating its riches and wiping out its plantations. . . . The United States has been occupying the lands of Islam in the holiest of places, the Arabian Peninsula, plundering its riches, dictating to its rulers, humiliating its people, terrorizing its neighbors, and turning its bases in the Peninsula into a spearhead through which to fight the neighboring Muslim peoples. . . . The ruling to kill Americans and their allies—civilian and military—is an individual duty for every

Muslim, in order to liberate the al-Aqsa Mosque [in Jerusalem]
and the Holy Mosque [in Mecca] from their grip and in order for
their armies, defeated, to move out of all the lands of Islam.[9]

His goal, bin Laden declared, was both to drive America from
the Islamic homeland and to replace the Sauds with a regime
of Islamic purity.

Bin Laden opened his offensive against the infidels in 1993,
when al-Qaeda agents, in what was later recognized as a test
run, exploded a truck bomb underground in New York's
World Trade Center. In succeeding years, al-Qaeda repeatedly bombed American military installations in Saudi Arabia.
It also bombed the American embassies in Kenya and Tanza-
nia, and an American naval destroyer docked in Yemen. In
these attacks, he indiscriminately killed Muslims, as well as
Christians and Jews.

Though it had by now identified bin Laden as a terrorist,
the United States, uncertain about his intentions, retaliated
only sporadically. In 1998 it fired missiles that struck al-
Qaeda training camps in Afghanistan, as well as a chemical
factory in Sudan that was alleged to be under bin Laden's
management. The retaliation did little damage. Bin Laden
survived, as did the al-Qaeda organization and its host, the
Taliban. If anything, the U.S. attacks elevated bin Laden's
stature among Arabs and helped speed Islamic radicalization
within the Arab world.

Then, on September 11, 2001, al-Qaeda, in a spectacular
suicide attack, hijacked four American airliners and crashed
two of them into the World Trade Center, in New York, and
a third into the Pentagon, in Washington. The fourth crashed
in a field in Pennsylvania.

These attacks are likely to go down as a watershed in the
West's relations with the Arab world. The New York target
was selected as a quintessential symbol of America's civiliza-

tion, the Washington target as the symbol of its military power. The attacks, in evading the efforts of intelligence agencies and military defenses, were recognized by Americans, however grudgingly, as having been brilliantly organized and executed. Yet they did little long-term damage to the United States, and it remains puzzling what service—other than the gratification of historic revenge—they could have rendered to the Arabs or to Islam.

The September 11 attacks elevated the long-standing tensions between the Arab world and the West. Though Western leaders—most notably President Bush—have stated repeatedly that their quarrel is with terrorism, not with Islam, official wariness toward Arabs and Arab states has soared. Muslims living in the West feel themselves far more vulnerable than before. The widespread Arab reticence to criticize bin Laden publicly has made matters only worse. The breach between the two civilizations has broadened drastically since September 11 and does not seem likely to narrow at any time soon.

President Bush, having announced soon after the attack that bin Laden was responsible, declared a "war on terror." It is a measure of the Arabs' mistrust that so few accepted bin Laden's culpability and changed their minds only after he himself boasted of the bombings. Bush dispatched an army to Afghanistan to destroy bin Laden and his sanctuary. Unable to find him, the army leveled the Taliban regime, erecting in its place a Western-style, parliamentary state. The state, however, has scarcely surpassed its predecessors in overcoming the divisions that remain intrinsic to Afghan society.

Not satisfied with his measures in Afghanistan, Bush announced that an even greater danger lay in Iraq. Saddam's regime possessed weapons of mass destruction and was collaborating with bin Laden in spreading terror, he declared. International security required "regime change," Bush said.

Even America's traditional allies were skeptical of his claims, except for Kuwait, and Iraq's neighbors declined to join him in proclaiming Saddam a threat. The president, however, refused to retreat from the decision to invade Iraq.

Among the allies who had participated in the first Bush's war against Saddam, America received major support only from Britain. Reticence particularly characterized the Arab states, which perceived the two wars very differently. If Arab involvement in the war of 1991 could be justified as the defense of Arab sovereignty against Iraqi aggression, the war of 2003 looked to most Arabs like a fresh expression of old-fashioned Western imperialism.

When I visited Iraq on the eve of the American attack, Iraqis said to me, Yes, Saddam Hussein is a scoundrel, but he is *our* scoundrel; he is our problem to deal with, not yours. To many Arabs, the war on Iraq appeared to be America's effort not to save the world from Saddam Hussein but to preserve its own oil interests, project its power globally, and remake the Middle East in its own image. Even many non-Arabs adopted this view.

For the second time, American forces in 2003 invaded Iraq from bases in Saudi Arabia. Successful in their early battles, in which their superior technology prevailed, they were soon confronted with a guerrilla insurgency, a type of warfare at which the Arabs have historically excelled. During World War I, Faisal's Bedouins beat the Turks in guerrilla war. Between the World Wars, Europe's two great empires were scarcely able to contain guerrilla conflicts in Syria and Iraq. The French lost Algeria in 1962 after years of guerrilla war. Farther afield, guerrillas in Afghanistan brought down the Soviet Union. The Arab guerrillas in Iraq confounded the American troops.

Iraq's insurgency was maddening to the Americans in that it seemed to have no central leadership, and even its goals were unclear. As American casualties rose, Sunnis and Shi'ites were increasingly targeting each other. When Shi'ites began to acquire political benefits from the occupation, the insurgency took on a more Sunni tilt. Still, within an emerging struggle for power among Iraqis, insurgents and noninsurgents seemed to share Arab nationalism's opposition to the U.S. occupation. In fact, in the occupation's wake, Arab nationalism appeared to be all that Iraqis had in common.

In embracing suicide as a tactic, the insurgents were driven by an Arab vision which held that no sacrifice was too great to expel the Crusaders, the intruders from the Christian West. They imposed most of the sacrifice, in indiscriminate bombing, on innocent Iraqi civilians, yet popular opposition to the insurgency was slow to develop. Instead, reports of American mistreatment of Iraqis in interrogations—brutal torture, arbitrary imprisonment, sexual humiliation, religious desecration—fanned Arab nationalism's flames. On the anniversary of the fall of the Ba'athi regime in 2005, tens of thousands of Iraqis marched through Baghdad's streets shouting, "No Saddam, no America." In their hostility to Western interlopers, all Iraqis seemed to be declaring that they were nationalists.

EPILOGUE

As 2005 ground to an end, President Bush reacted to the grim reports coming from the urban battlefields of Iraq by channeling an undercurrent of personal despair, only recently acknowledged, into increasingly shrill predictions of ultimate victory.

The political remedies that the occupation authorities ordered throughout 2005 to frame a replacement for the Saddam regime—the election of a provisional assembly in January, the adoption of a constitution in October, the election of a parliament in December—had failed to produce the harmony that the president had predicted for them. It was not that Iraqis, suspicious as they were of Western democracy, rejected the electoral process; on the contrary, they went to the polls in great numbers. But the numbers concealed the real story. Iraqis, having learned that they could promote their communal interests at the ballot box, turned the tables on the occupiers, producing disturbing consequences for which the United States had not prepared.

Democracy, despite the president's claims for it, may not be exportable; it is surely not, at least now, Iraq's cup of tea. To succeed, democracy requires individuals to make their own judgments. Sectarianism, tribalism, and regionalism are its enemies. Americans in 1860 voted in huge numbers, too, only to prove that their regional differences were irreconcilable; the 1860 election ignited America's tragic Civil War. Similarly, Iraq's election of 2005 was a triumph of sectarianism, in which few Iraqis voted as individuals. Shi'ites voted as Shi'ites, Sunnis as Sunnis, Kurds as Kurds. Because 60 percent of Iraqis are Shi'ite, the Shi'ite parties won overwhelmingly. The elections provided no advancement toward a stable society; in fact, they gave warning of precisely the opposite.

The election conveyed to Kurds, who had always resented becoming part of Iraq by fiat of the Allies after World War I, that the sovereign state they sought was, through effective secession, within their grasp. While President Bush boasted of the newly organized Iraqi military, assuring constituents that it would take over security duties from American GIs, Kurdish militias inside Iraq's army—like their Shi'ite counterparts—were gearing up to serve sectarian interests. The Kurdish target was the disputed city of Kirkuk, regarded as the key to the oil riches of the Iraqi north, which both Kurds and Sunni Arabs claimed as their own.

In contrast to the Kurds, Sunnis considered themselves preeminently Iraqi—the *real* Iraqis. Since Ottoman times they had dominated Iraqi politics. As they saw it, the American-crafted democracy was a zero-sum contest that doomed them to political irrelevance. To be sure, majoritarian decision-making is the essence of democracy. But Sunni unwillingness to play second fiddle in Iraq virtually guaranteed civil conflict. At best, it was likely to produce a society of diverse fragments in perpetual disorder.

To Shi'ites, the election was an instrument for settling scores, offering retribution for their long history of forced submission to the Sunnis. Traditionally religious, most Shi'ites were disposed to theocratic rule; most Sunnis, far more secular, were horrified at the prospect. Shi'ites were no less outraged than Sunnis by America's invasion, but, realizing that the occupation served a political objective that was unattainable under Saddam, they were content to let Sunnis take the initiative in the anti-American resistance.

As the year 2006 opened, the pattern of the insurgency left little doubt that, while Shi'ites were not acquiescing to the American occupation and Kurds were walking away, Sunnis were rising up to challenge the emerging political system. This marked a change from a year or two earlier, when observers blamed the violence on al-Qaeda, or on a remnant of loyalists of Saddam Hussein. Both were still involved in the fighting, but it was hardly deniable now that the bulk of the rebels were Sunnis struggling to preserve a place in Iraq's political culture. Though Washington stated repeatedly that the insurgency was in its death throes, without a Sunni-Shi'ite settlement the violence was clearly going to continue, and probably would grow worse.

Oddly, President Bush appeared unaware of the strategic implications of Shi'ite hegemony. Iraq's new army was heavily Shi'ite, dominated by militias under clerical command. The emerging state resembled Khomeini's Iran, in which clerics supported by funds from Tehran would rule with indifference to political freedoms and women's rights. Though Bush might ignore the trespasses of American principles, he would have to face the dangers of Iraq's embrace of a member of the "axis of evil." Thanks to the invasion, the president was helping to transform Iran, his implacable foe, into a significant power. It was a curious conception of the "victory" he promised.

In December, after the election, the president sought to reassure American listeners by declaring that the "new Iraq shares our deepest values." To be sure, President Bush, who had ordered Iraq's invasion on the grounds of Saddam's nonexistent weapons of mass destruction, was now famous worldwide for his carelessness with facts. Still, with insurgency raging and Iran growing more perverse, it seemed strange that he and his advisors had not yet learned that America's problems in the region started, precisely, from the Islamic community's sharply *contrasting* values, whether Sunni or Shi'ite.

Indeed, three years of war had demonstrated that America today is no more capable than was Britain a century ago of persuading the Arabs to accept the West's values. Britain, at least, had run its empire with professionals; America's leaders, by comparison, were untrained, often incompetent amateurs, oblivious to the acute animosity between East and West generated by fourteen centuries of history. Far from celebrating Saddam's overthrow as the president had predicted, Iraqi crowds, both Sunni and Shi'ite, roamed the streets daily denouncing the "crusaders." The invasion of Iraq has only widened the gap in values between the Arab world and the West.

—

In 1990, the Soviet Union's collapse had left the world with a single superpower, but the unique status this imparted to the United States did not confer upon it a capacity to act without regard for the concerns of other nations. America has since had to confront the lesson that even an unrivaled colossus must operate within a framework of inherent limitations. In seeking to conduct the nation's affairs otherwise, the Bush administration has made a serious conceptual error, imposing profound costs on America's interests.

The evidence of this error is widespread. Many of America's best friends, for example, have not forgiven its rejection of the authority of the United Nations in invading Iraq. America's self-exemption from the jurisdiction of international war crimes tribunals, and its insistence on special privileges in dealing with the environment, have left major scars. Its assertion, as a right of the "war on terrorism," of a power to seize suspects secretly within foreign borders has provoked outrage, even among NATO allies. The irate feelings go beyond policy matters; polls have shown that America, once hugely popular, has alienated people everywhere. But the loss of esteem has been especially acute in the Middle East, where American policies have seemed consistently brazen and sometimes irrational. Iraq was not unique.

After the 9/11 attacks, the United States had landed troops in Afghanistan to capture Osama bin Laden, the chief perpetrator. The operation received wide support, even among Muslims, and began promisingly. To nearly universal applause, the U.S. quickly overthrew the Taliban regime, which had supplied bin Laden with a sanctuary. The Bush administration, however, became distracted by its designs on Iraq and failed to give Afghanistan its full attention. The state it established in Kabul to replace the Taliban, though democratic, was never secure. While it tottered dangerously, the Taliban regrouped and the chance to seize bin Laden was lost.

In Iraq, America's invasion blanketed the terrain with heavily armed troops, but they had no preparation for dealing with guerrilla warfare. Despite the invaders' overwhelming firepower, it was the insurgents who dictated the terms of the fighting, using tactics at which they excelled. They fought much like the Arabs of the previous century who struggled for freedom from colonialism. They avoided pitched battles, conducting hit-and-run actions in which the loss of lives, though a few at a time, was relentless. The insurgency imposed huge monetary costs and tied down an army of 150,000 men, the bulk of America's available strength. The positive side of the failure to impose order in Iraq may, ironically, have been to save the Bush administration from blundering into equally costly operations in Syria and Iran.

America's initial high-tech successes delivered a false message. The army celebrated by toppling Saddam's statue in downtown Baghdad, but it was unable to contain the looting on Iraq's streets. Having massively bombed Iraq's infrastructure, the U.S. fell short in getting food to the hungry and medical treatment to the sick; it also failed to restore fuel supplies, potable water, and electric power. It disbanded Iraq's army and police forces, offering the insurgency a pool of angry unemployed recruits. It authorized a free press, then suppressed the newspapers and television that criticized it. It called for a commitment to human rights but was revealed as a massive abuser of Iraqi prisoners at Abu Ghraib.

In an imperfect world, it is clear there is no *good* military occupation. But the American occupation of Iraq was far worse than it should have been.

President Bush defended the occupation as an indispensable instrument in the war on terror, but even that claim was probably untrue. The Iraq war did not stop deadly terrorist acts in London, Madrid, Amman, or even distant Bali. The president's fall in the polls, moreover, suggested that the war had eroded the sense of security of Americans at home.

Meanwhile, religious extremism in the Muslim world surged. In elections in 2005, Iran replaced a moderate president with a militant Islamist; Egypt's Muslim Brotherhood became the principal opposition force in the parliament; in Lebanon, Hezbollah, an anti-Western Shi'ite party, won enough mandates to claim two seats in the cabinet. In Iraq, meanwhile, the American-led elections provided Shi'ite extremists with the invitation to press for an Islamic state; even some Sunni clerics supported the idea.

An obvious step available to Washington to slow the momentum toward Islamic radicalism was to direct its power toward resolving the Israeli-Palestinian conflict. Dating back to Sykes-Picot and the Balfour Declaration in the World War I era, the idea of a Jewish "homeland" evoked deep feelings of injustice among Arabs. President Bush had pronounced himself, in principle, in favor of old-style partition, which would produce an independent Palestinian state; he even proposed a "roadmap" to statehood, which in theory Israeli prime minister Sharon endorsed. But Palestinians remained under Israeli rule and nearly all Arabs, perceiving Israel as America's agent, held America responsible.

Notwithstanding the "roadmap," under President Bush the United States put little effort into modifying the status quo in Palestine. That Israel, in withdrawing Jewish settlements from Gaza in 2005, imparted no momentum to the peace process marked another lost opportunity. The conflict raged on, with Palestinians and Israelis blaming each other for the ongoing loss of innocent lives. With or without Iraq, Washington's passivity in Palestine would have kept the Arabs' anti-Americanism alive.

Meanwhile, the rise of Islamic extremism on the Bush watch gave Palestinian politics a more ominous color. Hamas, a radical Islamic movement that descended from Egypt's Muslim Brothers, rejected Israel's existence outright and emerged as a significant political force. Designating it a terrorist organization, America placed Hamas on its boycott list, which only legitimized it for Palestinian voters. After Hamas won control of several major municipalities in local elections in December 2005, Israel sought unsuccessfully to bar it from further political involvement. In the election of January 2006, Hamas won nearly two thirds of the seats in parliament, a shocking defeat for Washington as well as Israel. The outcome not only cast doubt on President Bush's democratic vows but placed the prospect for a peaceful resolution to the Arab-Israeli conflict at a greater distance than ever.

In retrospect, it is clear President Bush would have served his country better by circumscribing his response to the attacks on 9/11. Had he limited retaliation to Osama bin Laden and al-Qaeda in Afghanistan, he would have made a credible case, even among Arabs. Instead, without evidence of the attacks being linked in any way to Iraq's government, he sent a huge army to Iraq and even threatened Syria, whose ties to bin Laden were equally tenuous. He still threatens Iran. Arabs saw the president's "war on terrorism" as an assault on the Islamic heartland. Though President Bush repeatedly stated that his quarrel was not with Islam, what Arabs saw was a fierce American belligerence, which they inevitably placed into the context of the ancient conflict between Islamic civilization and the West.

———

Nothing in this book is meant to convey the message that there is a quick remedy to erase this ancient antagonism between East and West. It is too deeply entrenched for that. The problem is not that Christians and Jews worship God differently from Muslims, though that may be a small part. More significant, during the centuries in which the two civilizations have been rivals, one drifted increasingly toward humanism, secularism, and materialism, while the other remained essentially faithful to community, worship, and the hereafter. Moreover, the West's military superiority exploited the East's weakness through the practice of an imperialism that reached its pinnacle in the twentieth century and has not yet run its full course.

The gap between West and East is now wider than ever, but what 9/11 and its aftermath have shown is that each side retains weapons that can inflict significant damage on the other. The damage lies less in the rubble, however, which can be swept away with a broom, than in the collective soul, where the poison of hatred lodges. Based on what has ensued since the Trade Center towers fell, it is clear that both sides have suffered from inflaming the conflict. Would not West as well as East profit from putting its energy into bridging the divide?

Iraq is presently the most flammable arena of the conflict,

but in overreacting there America has not made the West safer. Not only is terrorism deadlier; no less important, in an era of exploding population and technology, Arab migration has seeded restless societies in the West, where Arab warriors are positioned conveniently for terrorism. It is also clear that America's presence on Arab lands serves in itself as incitement. U.S. forces are deployed not just in Iraq but in Saudi Arabia, Jordan, Kuwait, Bahrain, Qatar, Yemen, and Egypt. Bin Laden says American bases near Islam's holy sites are his biggest grievance. One scholar, after careful research, concludes that al-Qaeda's terrorism aims not so much at promoting fundamentalism but at driving Americans from Arab soil.[1]

Yet America, in the face of this grievance, shows no sign of withdrawing its armed forces from the Arab world. President Bush's strategy, in fact, is to increase the military's global reach. One prospect is that the United States will be fighting more wars like that in Iraq in the future. It is true that the curve of public opinion since the Iraq invasion suggests that Americans do not like a strategy of recurring conflict. As a result, the president has been forced to acknowledge that at some point the army has to go, but he insists it will not be before he can leave behind a viable democratic regime. If America must first defeat the insurgency and clean up the political mess that the invasion created, however, the wait may be very long indeed.

As we enter the year 2006, the gravest peril looming in Iraq is that the insurgency will turn into a full-scale civil war, even bloodier than what is currently under way, with Sunnis fighting with Shi'ites and maybe with Kurds. The United States faces the peril of being unable to extricate itself from such a conflict. The Arab states would have even more at stake in such a war, since it may spread beyond Iraq's borders to ignite the powder of regional instability. And beyond the Middle East, a peril lies in the unforeseeable consequences of an out-of-control conflagration, which could include the weapons of mass destruction that Saddam Hussein never had but which other Muslims do.

Despite its 150,000 troops in Iraq, the Bush administration is not equipped to head off this war. The president's strategy is based on an ignorance of the dynamics of Iraq and the Arab world, and he has staked his personal prestige on a victory for which the prospects are slim. Pleas by his representatives to Iraq's factional leaders to reconcile their differences fall on deaf ears. Instinctively, they regard Americans as crusaders from across the seas, as meddlers in Iraqi affairs. This attitude has left America with military muscle but no moral power. Unable to control the forces of disorder, Americans can kill but they cannot stop the killing, leaving them without a plan either for winning or withdrawing.

The solution may well lie with the president's willingness to turn to the Arab community for help. The Arab states, every one of them volatile, recognize the jeopardy they themselves face in Iraq. A shattered Iraq would reverberate on all of them. Whatever their resentment of American intrusion into their affairs, the Arab states now share with America an interest in keeping Iraq's society and territorial integrity intact.

The Arab League can bring its collective authority to the problem. It is true that the Arab League has historically been a weakling, even when measured against other international bodies. Its members mistrust one another and often squabble. But it has risen to the challenge before to rescue one of its members from the brink of disintegration. The threat the Arabs perceived to themselves at that time was an incentive that overcame their inherent divisions.

The occasion was Lebanon, which had been engaged since 1975 in a seemingly intractable civil war. Lebanon's Christians, Druzes, Sunnis, and Shi'ites, along with its Palestinian refugees, were butchering one another mercilessly. In 1983,

President Reagan offered a peace plan, which he bolstered by sending in a contingent of Marines, but the Lebanese, fearful of reopening a door to imperialism, would have nothing to do with him; Reagan, after a suicide bombing killed 241 of them, brought the Marines home. For a few years, the Lebanese, in despair, wondered whether the only way to stop the violence would be to divide the country among the factions. None of the factions, however, not even the Christians, wanted partition. Exhausted as they were, the factions retained a common vision—as most Iraqis do today—of a unified nation.

In January 1989, the Arab League designated a team of six foreign ministers to come up with a solution. Though some Arab states grumbled at being left out, the ministers worked diligently to reach an accord, which an Arab League summit proceeded to endorse. The summit assigned the Saudi and Moroccan kings and the president of Algeria the task of hammering out an agreement among the Lebanese. This "troika" put Lakhdar Ibrahimi, an Algerian diplomat, in charge. It might be noted that, fifteen years later, the same Ibrahimi arrived in Baghdad as the UN representative for peacemaking in Iraq, but America's occupation authorities, disdainful of UN meddling, made his work impossible. In 1989, however, the Lebanese welcomed him.

Ibrahimi spoke as an Arab to Arabs, with the moral authority of the Arab world; the Lebanese listened. In September 1989, he negotiated a cease-fire among Lebanon's warring factions, then convoked the Lebanese parliament in Taif, a Saudi mountain town, for a meeting under the troika's sponsorship. Presiding was Saud al-Faisal, the Saudi foreign minister, a skilled diplomat who today promotes a comparable reconciliation between Iraq's factions.

After three weeks of intense bargaining, all the Lebanese factions retreated from positions they had vowed never to give up, and signed an accord based on the Arab League draft.

It must be acknowledged that Taif did not produce a perfect ending. Given Lebanon's fragility, such an ending would have been too much to expect. But, to widespread surprise, the rule of parliament was restored and, though violence persists, Lebanese life has since become relatively normal.

Is there a lesson for President Bush in Taif? The Arab League met again in Cairo in November 2005, and sent signals conveying a willingness to step into negotiations. In Iraq, voices from within the insurgency have suggested an interest in going along. In fact, reports indicate that indigenous Sunni insurgents have clashed repeatedly over the issue with foreign terrorists, most of them affiliated with al-Qaeda. What is more, some of President Bush's officers in the field, and even his ambassador, have let it be known that they regard a political settlement as more sensible than prolonging an unwinnable fight.

Key to the success of the negotiations at Taif was the absence of foreign interference. Taif was conducted outside the framework of the Cold War and the United Nations. It was an all-Arab affair. Ending Lebanon's civil war was an Arab triumph.

Is President Bush man enough to defer to the Arabs and allow them such a triumph in Iraq? The Arabs would be unlikely to undertake the task with American officials hovering over them. Inviting the Arabs in, however, contains a promise not only of peace in Iraq but of stability in the Middle East. Is this not what the president wants? Is this not what the world wants? The alternative would be that history, taking note of the inexhaustible antagonism between Arab civilization and the West, remembers the Bush administration for pouring fuel upon the struggle.

Washington, D.C.
February 1, 2006

SOURCES

This is a work of historical interpretation, rooted in more than three decades of my own reporting in the Middle East and in my reading over the years of countless volumes on the history, religion, and politics of the region. Much of the narrative that derives directly from my experience is recorded in my earlier books, though often in different contexts. These books are cited in the Bibliography. Information that has been absorbed into my personal memory, from books I may have long ago forgotten, I have tried to recheck against either my own or others' works.

In preparing the manuscript, I was well served by two comprehensive histories, George Lenczowski's *The Middle East in World Affairs* and William L. Cleveland's *A History of the Modern Middle East*. I also returned to such classics as George Antonius's *The Arab Awakening* and Philip K. Hitti's *History of the Arabs*, as well as to the many books of Bernard Lewis.

I have generally not footnoted information that is widely familiar. I have tried to provide footnotes for less well-known facts, as well as for material from more narrowly focused works, such as Philip Khoury's noteworthy *Syria and the French Mandate*.

I am grateful to those who have read the manuscript, who have not only provided me with critical judgments but have also saved me from factual errors. They include Joyce Anderson, William Cleveland, Cvijeto Job, Philip Mattar, Richard Parker, Leslie Whitten, and my wife, Judy.

I take full responsibility, of course, for the information, as well as the interpretations, that the book contains.

NOTES

I. MEMORY, 622–1900

1. Ron Suskind, "Without a Doubt," *New York Times Magazine*, October 17, 2004.

2. Daryl Champion, *The Paradoxical Kingdom: Saudi Arabia and the Momentum of Reform* (New York: Columbia University Press, 2003), p. 64.

3. Ibn Khaldun, *The Muqaddimah: An Introduction to History* (Princeton: Princeton University Press, 1969), pp. 121–22.

4. Adeed Dawisha, *Arab Nationalism in the Twentieth Century: From Triumph to Despair* (Princeton: Princeton University Press, 2003), p. 219.

5. Cited by F. E. Peters, *Muhammad and the Origins of Islam* (Albany: SUNY Press, 1994), p. 23.

6. *Report of the Defense Science Board Task Force on Strategic Communication* (Washington, D.C.: Office of the Undersecretary of Defense for Acquisition, Technology and Logistics, September 2004), p. 36.

7. See Samuel P. Huntington, *The Clash of Civilizations and the Remaking of World Order* (New York: Simon & Schuster, 1996).

8. Ibn Khaldun, *Muqaddimah*, p. 183.

9. Edward Gibbon, *History of the Decline and Fall of the Roman Empire* (London: Everyman Library, 1900), vol. 6, p. 15.

10. Bernard Lewis, *Islam and the West* (New York: Oxford University Press, 1993), p. 17.

11. J. C. Hurewitz, *Diplomacy in the Near and Middle East: A Documentary Record* (Princeton: Van Nostrand, 1956), vol. 2, 1914–1956, p. 63.

II. REVOLT, 1901–1918

1. Randall Baker, *King Husain and the Kingdom of Hejaz* (New York: Oleander, 1979), pp. 6–16.
2. George Antonius, *The Arab Awakening* (New York: Capricorn, 1965), p. 169.
3. Ibid. Antonius's narrative, pp. 164–83; documents, pp. 413–27.
4. Joshua Teitelbaum, *The Rise and Fall of the Hashemite Kingdom of Arabia* (New York: New York University Press, 2001), pp. 104–6.
5. T. E. Lawrence, *The Seven Pillars of Wisdom* (New York: Penguin, 1979), p. 92.
6. Ibid., pp. 104–5
7. Antonius, *Arab Awakening,* narrative, pp. 244–53; document, pp. 428–30.
8. Ibid.; narrative, pp. 286–94; document, pp. 433–34.
9. Ibid., pp. 431–32.
10. Ibid., pp. 255–56.
11. Lawrence, *Seven Pillars,* p. 668.
12. Antonius, *Arab Awakening,* p. 238.
13. Lawrence, *Seven Pillars,* p. 53.

III. DISILLUSION, 1919–1939

1. John Maynard Keynes, *The Economic Consequences of the Peace* (New York: Harcourt Brace, 1920), p. 42.
2. Margaret MacMillan, *Paris 1919: Six Months That Changed the World* (New York: Random House, 2003), p. 11.
3. Antonius, *Arab Awakening,* narrative, pp. 288, 294–98, document, pp. 443–58.
4. Ibid., pp. 292–95; also David Fromkin, *A Peace to End All Peace: Creating the Modern Middle East, 1914–1922* (New York: Holt, 1989), pp. 435–36.
5. Naguib Mahfouz, *Palace Walk* (New York: Doubleday, 1990), pp. 347–48.
6. John Keay, *Sowing the Wind: The Seeds of Conflict in the Middle East* (New York: Norton, 2003), pp. 167–91; also Philip Khoury, *Syria*

and the French Mandate: The Politics of Arab Nationalism (Princeton: Princeton University Press, 1987), pp. 151–493.

7. John Norton Moore ed., *The Arab-Israeli Conflict: Readings and Documents* (Princeton: Princeton University Press, 1977), Balfour document, pp. 884–85; mandate document, pp. 891–901.

8. Tom Segev, *One Palestine, Complete: Jews and Arabs Under the British Mandate* (New York: Holt, 1999), pp. 121–41.

9. Baker, *King Husain,* pp. 204–5.

IV. Emancipation, 1940–1956

1. The classic study of the brotherhood is Richard P. Mitchell, *The Society of Muslim Brothers* (London: Oxford University Press, 1969).

2. Phebe Marr, *The Modern History of Iraq* (Boulder: Colo.: Westview, 1985), pp. 102–6.

3. Notwithstanding the voluminous research on Israeli history done since its publication, still unsurpassed as a source is Howard Sachar, *A History of Israel: From the Rise of Zionism to Our Time* (New York: Knopf, 1979), pp. 249–347.

4. Dawisha, *Arab Nationalism,* p. 124.

5. P. J. Vatikiotis, *Nasser and His Generation* (New York: St. Martin's, 1978), pp. 23–60.

6. Dawisha, *Arab Nationalism,* pp. 218–19.

V. Unity-Disunity, 1957–1967

1. William R. Polk, *The United States and the Arab World* (Cambridge, Mass: Harvard University Press, 1975), pp. 282–83.

2. Patrick Seale, *The Struggle for Syria* (New Haven: Yale University Press, 1987), pp. 283–326.

3. Thomas A. Bryson, *Tars, Turks and Tankers: The Role of the United States Navy in the Middle East, 1800–1979* (Metuchen, N.J.: Scarecrow, 1980), p. 130.

4. Marr, *Modern History of Iraq,* pp. 116–27, 153–90.

5. Dawisha, *Arab Nationalism,* pp. 234–37.

VI. THEOCRATS-AUTOCRATS, 1968–2005

1. Said K. Aburish, *Arafat: From Defender to Dictator* (London: Bloomsbury, 1998), pp. 7–67.
2. Anwar Sadat, *In Search of Identity* (New York: Harper & Row, 1978), pp. 1–24.
3. Daniel Yergin, *The Prize: The Epic Quest for Oil, Money, and Power* (New York: Simon & Schuster, 1991), pp. 588–632.
4. On the war in Afghanistan, see Peter W. Rodman, *More Precious Than Peace: The Cold War and the Struggle for the Third World* (New York: Scribner's, 1993), pp. 216–21, 324–57.
5. Peter Marsden, *The Taliban: War and Religion in Afghanistan* (New York: Zed, 2002), pp. 8–67.
6. Ibid., pp. 146–49; Peter L. Bergen, *Holy War, Inc.: Inside the Secret World of Osama bin Laden* (New York: Free Press, 2001), pp. 1–220.
7. Thomas W. Lippman, *Inside the Mirage: America's Fragile Partnership with Saudi Arabia* (Cambridge, Mass.: Westview, 2004), pp. 34, 105, 274–79.
8. Ibid., p. 316.
9. Robert A. Pape, *Dying to Win: The Strategic Logic of Suicide Terrorism* (New York: Random House, 2005), p. 54.

EPILOGUE

1. Robert A. Pape, *Dying to Win: The Strategic Logic of Suicide Terrorism* (New York: Random House, 2005). Pape presents evidence to support this thesis throughout his book. See also Pape, *New York Times* op-ed, July 9, 2005.

BIBLIOGRAPHY

Abdallah. *My Memoirs Completed*. London: Longman, 1978.
Abrahamian, Ervand. *Khomeinism*. Berkeley: University of California Press, 1993.
Aburish, Said K. *Arafat: From Defender to Dictator*. London: Bloomsbury, 1998.
———. *Nasser: The Last Arab*. New York: St. Martin's Press, 2004.

Antonius, George. *The Arab Awakening*. New York: Capricorn, 1965.

Arjomand, Said Amir. *The Turban for the Crown*. New York: Oxford University Press, 1988.

Baker, Randall. *King Husain and the Kingdom of Hejaz*. New York: Oleander, 1979.

Bergen, Peter L. *Holy War Inc.: Inside the Secret World of Osama bin Laden*. New York: Free Press, 2001.

Bill, James A. *The Eagle and the Lion: The Tragedy of American-Iranian Relations*. New Haven: Yale University Press, 1988.

Birdwell, Robin. Introduction to *Arabian Personalities of the Early Twentieth Century*. New York: Oleander, 1917.

Bryson, Thomas A. *Tars, Turks and Tankers: The Role of the United States Navy in the Middle East, 1800–1979*. Metuchen, N.J.: Scarecrow, 1980.

Champion, Daryl. *The Paradoxical Kingdom: Saudi Arabia and the Momentum of Reform*. New York: Columbia University Press, 2003.

Cleveland, William L. *A History of the Modern Middle East*. 3rd ed. Boulder, Colo.: Westview, 2004.

Dawisha, Adeed. *Arab Nationalism in the Twentieth Century: From Triumph to Despair*. Princeton: Princeton University Press, 2003.

Dawn, C. Ernest. *From Ottomanism to Arabism*. Urbana: University of Illinois Press, 1973.

Djait, Hichem. *Europe and Islam*. Berkeley: University of California Press, 1985.

Fontaine, Andre. *History of the Cold War*. Vol. 1, *From the October Revolution to the Korean War, 1917–1950*; vol. 2, *From the Korean War to the Present*. New York: Pantheon, 1968, 1969.

Freedman, Lawrence, and Efraim Karsh. *The Gulf Conflict, 1990–1991*. Princeton: Princeton University Press, 1993.

Fromkin, David. *A Peace to End All Peace: Creating the Modern Middle East, 1914–1922*. New York: Holt, 1989.

Gabrieli, Francesco. *Arab Historians of the Crusades*. New York: Dorset, 1989.

Gellner, Ernest. *Nations and Nationalism*. Ithaca: Cornell University Press, 1983.

Gibbon, Edward. *History of the Decline and Fall of the Roman Empire.* London: Everyman Library, 1900.

Haim, Sylvia. *Arab Nationalism.* Berkeley: University of California Press, 1976.

Hall, John A. *The State of the Nation: Ernest Gellner and the Theory of Nationalism.* Cambridge: Cambridge University Press, 1988.

Heikal, Mohamed. *The Cairo Documents.* New York: Doubleday, 1975.

Helms, Christine. *Iraq: The Eastern Flank of the Arab World.* Washington, D.C.: Brookings Institution, 1984.

Hitti, Philip K. *History of the Arabs.* New York: St. Martin's, 1970.

Huntington, Samuel P. *The Clash of Civilizations and the Remaking of World Order.* New York: Simon & Schuster, 1996.

Hurewitz, J. C. *Diplomacy in the Near and Middle East: A Documentary Record.* 2 vols. Princeton: Van Nostrand, 1956.

Ibn Khaldun. *The Muqaddimah: An Introduction to History.* Princeton: Princeton University Press, 1969.

Itzkowitz, Norman. *Ottoman Empire and Islamic Tradition.* Chicago: University of Chicago Press, 1972.

Keay, John. *Sowing the Wind: The Seeds of Conflict in the Middle East.* New York: Norton, 2003.

Keddie, Nikki. *An Islamic Response to Imperialism.* Berkeley: University of California Press, 1968.

Keynes, John Maynard. *The Economic Consequences of the Peace.* New York: Harcourt Brace, 1920.

Khadduri, Majid. *The Gulf War.* New York: Oxford University Press, 1988.

———, and Edmund Ghareeb. *War in the Gulf, 1990–91.* New York: Oxford University Press, 1997.

Khalidi, Rashid. *Resurrecting Empire: Western Footprints and America's Perilous Path in the Middle East.* Boston: Beacon Press, 2004.

Khoury, Philip. *Syria and the French Mandate: The Politics of Arab Nationalism.* Princeton: Princeton University Press, 1987.

Kohn, Hans. *Nationalism: Its Meaning and History.* New York: Van Nostrand, 1965.

Lacey, Robert. *The Kingdom of Saudi Arabia and the House of Saud.* New York: Harcourt Brace Jovanovich, 1981.

Laroui, Abdallah. *The Crisis of the Arab Intellectual.* Berkeley: University of California Press, 1976.

Lawrence, T. E. *The Seven Pillars of Wisdom.* New York: Penguin, 1979.

Lenczowski, George. *The Middle East in World Affairs.* Ithaca: Cornell University Press, 1980.

Lewis, Bernard. *The Arabs in History.* New York: Harper & Row, 1966.

———. *Islam and the West.* New York: Oxford University Press, 1993.

———. *The Middle East: A Brief History of the Last 2,000 Years.* New York: Scribner's, 1995.

Lippman, Thomas W. *Inside the Mirage: America's Fragile Partnership with Saudi Arabia.* Cambridge, Mass.: Westview, 2004.

Lunt, James. *Hussein of Jordan.* New York: Morrow, 1989.

Maalouf, Amin. *The Crusades Through Arab Eyes.* New York: Schocken, 1985.

Macdonald, Robert W. *The League of Arab States.* Princeton: Princeton University Press, 1965.

Mackey, Sandra. *The Saudis: Inside the Desert Kingdom.* New York: Houghton Mifflin, 1987.

MacMillan, Margaret. *Paris 1919: Six Months That Changed the World.* New York: Random House, 2003.

Mahfouz, Naguib. *Palace Walk.* New York: Doubleday, 1990.

Marr, Phebe. *The Modern History of Iraq.* Boulder, Colo.: Westview, 1985.

Marsden, Peter. *The Taliban: War and Religion in Afghanistan.* New York: Zed, 2002.

Mitchell, Richard P. *The Society of Muslim Brothers.* London: Oxford University Press, 1969.

Moore, John Norton, ed. *The Arab-Israeli Conflict: Readings and Documents.* Princeton: Princeton University Press, 1977.

Morris, Benny. *The Birth of the Palestinian Refugee Problem, 1947–9.* Cambridge: Cambridge University Press, 1987.

Nuseibeh, Hazem Zaki. *The Ideas of Arab Nationalism.* Ithaca: Cornell University Press, 1959.

O'Brien, Conor Cruise. *God Land: Reflections on Religion and Nationalism.* Cambridge, Mass.: Harvard University Press, 1988.

Oren, Michael B. *Six Days of War: June 1967 and the Making of the Modern Middle East.* New York: Oxford University Press, 2002.

Pape, Robert A. *Dying to Win: The Strategic Logic of Suicide Terrorism.* New York: Random House, 2005.

Peters, F. E. *Muhammad and the Origins of Islam.* Albany: SUNY Press, 1994.

Pfaff, William. *The Wrath of Nations: Civilization and the Furies of Nationalism.* New York: Simon & Schuster, 1993.

Polk, William R. *The United States and the Arab World.* Cambridge, Mass.: Harvard University Press, 1975.

Rodman, Peter W. *More Precious Than Peace: The Cold War and the Struggle for the Third World.* New York: Scribner's, 1993.

Sachar, Howard. *A History of Israel: From the Rise of Zionism to Our Time.* New York: Knopf, 1979.

Sadat, Anwar. *In Search of Identity.* New York: Harper & Row, 1978.

Seale, Patrick. *The Struggle for Syria.* New Haven: Yale University Press, 1987.

Segev, Tom. *One Palestine, Complete: Jews and Arabs Under the British Mandate.* New York: Holt, 1999.

Shlaim, Avi. *The Politics of Partition: King Abdullah, the Zionists and Palestine, 1921–1951.* New York: Columbia University Press, 1990.

Simon, Reeva S. *Iraq Between the Two World Wars.* New York: Columbia University Press, 1986.

Smith, Anthony. *Nationalism: Theory, Ideology, History.* Cambridge, U.K.: Polity Press, 2001.

Teitelbaum, Joshua. *The Rise and Fall of the Hashemite Kingdom of Arabia.* New York: New York University Press, 2001.

Unger, Craig. *House of Bush, House of Saud.* New York: Scribner, 2004.

Vatikiotis, P. J. *Nasser and His Generation.* New York: St. Martin's, 1978.

Viorst, Milton. *In the Shadow of the Prophet: The Struggle for the Soul of Islam.* Boulder, Colo.: Westview, 2001.

———. *Reaching for the Olive Branch: UNRWA and Peace in the Middle East.* Bloomington: Indiana University Press, 1989.

———. *Sandcastles: The Arabs in Search of the Modern World.* New York: Knopf, 1994.

———. *Sands of Sorrow: Israel's Journey from Independence.* New York: Harper & Row, 1987.

Volkan, Vamik D., and Norman Itzkowitz. *The Immortal Ataturk.* Chicago: University of Chicago Press, 1987.

Wallach, Janet, and John Wallach. *Arafat.* New York: Lyle Stuart, 1989.

Yergin, Daniel. *The Prize: The Epic Quest for Oil, Money, and Power.* New York: Simon & Schuster, 1991.

Zeine, Zeine M. *Arab-Turkish Relations and the Emergence of Arab Nationalism.* Beirut: Khayat's, 1958.

INDEX

Page numbers in *italics* refer to the map on pages x–xi.

About the Author

MILTON VIORST has covered the Middle East as a journalist and scholar since the 1960s. He was *The New Yorker*'s Middle East correspondent, and his work has appeared in *The New York Times, The Washington Post*, the *Los Angeles Times,* and *The Wall Street Journal.* He has written six books on the Middle East, and lives in Washington, D.C., with his wife, the poet Judith Viorst.

A Note on the Type

The principal text of this Modern Library edition
was set in a digitized version of Janson, a typeface that
dates from about 1690 and was cut by Nicholas Kis,
a Hungarian working in Amsterdam. The original matrices have
survived and are held by the Stempel foundry in Germany.
Hermann Zapf redesigned some of the weights and sizes for
Stempel, basing his revisions on the original design.